ARMENIAN GENOCIDE

THE GREAT CRIME OF WORLD WAR I

DAVID CHARLWOOD

Pen & Sword
MILITARY

Русский: Памятная монета Армении
2015 года '100 лет геноциду армян'

Cover image: The bones of Armenians burned alive by Turkish soldiers in Sheykhalan, in the province of Mush. Discovered by Russian soldiers (pictured) in 1915.

First published in Great Britain in 2019 by
PEN AND SWORD MILITARY
an imprint of
Pen and Sword Books Ltd
47 Church Street
Barnsley
South Yorkshire S70 2AS

ISBN 978 1 52672 901 9

Map by George Anderson
Typeset by Aura Technology and Software Services, India
Printed and bound by CPI Group (UK) Ltd, Croydon, CR0 4YY

Pen & Sword Books Ltd incorporates the imprints of Pen & Sword
Archaeology, Atlas, Aviation, Battleground, Discovery, Family History, History, Maritime, Military,
Naval, Politics, Railways, Select, Social History, Transport, True Crime, Claymore Press, Frontline
Books, Leo Cooper, Praetorian Press, Remember When, Seaforth Publishing and Wharncliffe.

For a complete list of Pen and Sword titles please contact
Pen and Sword Books Limited
47 Church Street, Barnsley, South Yorkshire, S70 2AS, England
email: enquiries@pen-and-sword.co.uk
website: www.pen-and-sword.co.uk

CONTENTS

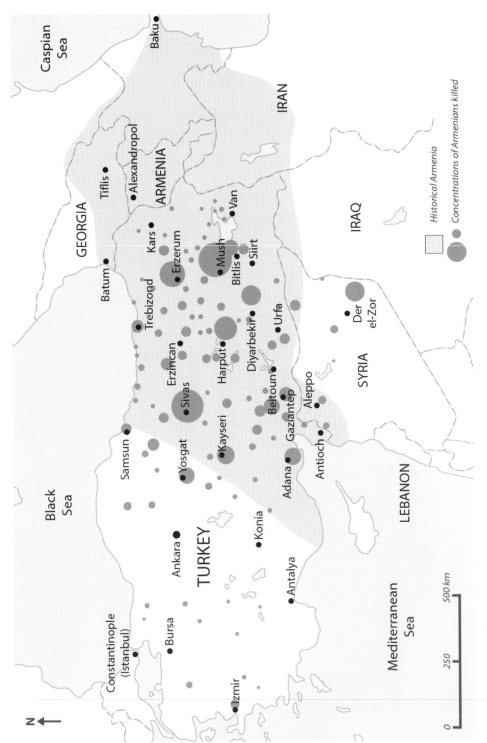

The Armenian Genocide.

4

INTRODUCTION

Hitler stood and addressed his generals: "In a few weeks hence I shall stretch out my hand ... to redistribute the world." If any of the men listening were still unsure of the violence of the Führer's ambitions, he quickly elaborated: "Genghis Khan has sent millions of women and children into death knowingly and with a light heart. History sees in him only as the great founder of States ... the goal to be obtained in the war is not that of reaching certain lines but of physically demolishing the opponent. And so for the present only in the East I have put my death-head formations in place with the command relentlessly and without compassion to send into death many women and children of Polish origin and language. Only thus we can gain the living space that we need." Hitler's justification, secretly noted down by Admiral Wilhelm Canaris, the head of German military intelligence, was simple: "Who after all is today speaking about the destruction of the Armenians?" It was 22 August 1939. Just over a week later, the German Blitzkrieg decimated Poland.

Hitler's speech, made to his commanders on the eve of war as they gathered at the Führer's Bavarian alpine retreat, was never intended to be made public, although it was later submitted as evidence at the Nuremberg Trials. His statement about "the destruction of the Armenians" was, in 1939, largely correct. The deaths of 1.5 million Armenians (as well as perhaps as many as a million Assyrians and Greeks) at the hands of the Ottoman-Turks two decades before seemed to have faded from the pages of history, remembered only by the scattered diaspora who had escaped the systematic slaughter and found refuge in Syria and parts of Europe. But the Armenian Genocide did not occur unnoticed. The U.S. ambassador to Ottoman-Turkey relayed unequivocal contemporary evidence of what was happening to the State Department, multiple eyewitness reports were supplied by missionaries, soldiers and diplomats, and the atrocities were publicly condemned by the governments of the United States, Russia, France and the United Kingdom. Perhaps one of the most remarkable aspects of the twentieth century's first genocide is how quickly it became convenient to forget it had ever happened. The Nazis would go on to murder millions of Jews in the most organized deliberate slaughter of humanity the world has ever seen, but the Holocaust is now commemorated worldwide: Auschwitz itself is a museum to the most horrific extremes of man's inhumanity to man and Holocaust Memorial Day is honoured

MILLION ARMENIANS KILLED OR IN EXILE

American Committee on Relief Says Victims of Turks Are Steadily Increasing.

POLICY OF EXTERMINATION

More Atrocities Detailed in Support of Charge That Turkey Is Acting Deliberately.

The New York Times, 15 December 1915.

internationally. The murder of six million Jews is not forgotten, but in modern-day Turkey, it is still a crime to remember publicly the genocide of the Armenians.

This short book seeks to tell the stories of those who died, as well as examine the efforts of diplomats from different countries who tried to dissuade key figures in the Turkish government from eradicating an entire race. Some parts of the story (including the genocide of the Assyrians and Greeks) have only been covered very briefly, while other elements have had to be excluded entirely for the sake of brevity. The central narrative follows the American ambassador Henry Morgenthau, who found himself thrust into a diplomatic crisis with no diplomatic experience. His humanity, and the humanity of others who helped and aided the Armenians, shines through in the midst of harrowing accounts from those who endured and witnessed unspeakable suffering.

The Armenian genocide remains an extremely contentious subject, in large part because the Turkish government refuses to acknowledge that it ever happened. Even many modern-day Turks remain sceptical of the numbers of those who are said to have been killed, or the systemic and murderous nature of their deaths. However, it is irrefutable that those who witnessed the atrocities were in absolutely no doubt about what was happening and contemporary reports of the massacre of a million people appeared in newspapers around the world. When, in 1917, a German engineer working in Turkey stumbled across a valley full of sun-bleached human bones, local villagers glibly affirmed that he had found an Armenian mass grave.

Traditionally, the start of the genocide is commemorated as April 1915, when Turkish authorities began rounding up Armenian notables. Soon after, Armenian communities were deported. Many of those who managed to survive the privations of travelling through the desert in the height of summer were then slaughtered en masse, having been stripped of all their possessions, including their clothes. Photographs of piles of naked bodies were smuggled out of the country and shocked the world when they appeared in the Western press. But despite some of the ring leaders facing trial for war crimes, the strong statements of intent to punish the perpetrators made by the victorious Powers of the First World War were swiftly overtaken by events. Less than half a decade after hundreds of thousands of Armenians were marched in convoys into the Syrian desert to be hacked to death, it suddenly became politically expedient to forget such events had taken place. It is little wonder therefore that the Armenian genocide was only the first of many in the twentieth century.

1. A NEW WORLD

On 27 November 1913, the United States' new ambassador to Turkey stepped off the train in Constantinople. "My first impression," he later wrote, "was of a moving sea of silk hats." Henry Morgenthau was fifty-seven years old. It was his first political appointment.

Morgenthau was not a seasoned diplomat. Born into a Jewish family in Mannheim, Germany, his parents had immigrated to the United States when he was nine years old. The young Morgenthau initially pursued a career in law and then made a fortune in real estate. His money brought political connections and Morgenthau was a major donor to Woodrow Wilson's successful 1912 presidential campaign. President Wilson repaid his generous friend with an ambassadorship.

On his way to Constantinople, Morgenthau crossed the Atlantic aboard the German-built liner the SS *George Washington* and visited London, Paris and Vienna before arriving at his posting. In 1913, Constantinople was the capital of an Ottoman Empire that stretched from the Black Sea coast to the sacred city of Mecca. The empire encompassed modern-day Iraq, Syria, Lebanon, Jordan, Israel, and Saudi Arabia's western coast, as well as what is now Turkey. Within its borders were multiple ethnic groups—Arabs, Armenians, Assyrians, Circassians, Kurds, Turks—but the official government censuses focused on only one thing: religion. A formal census was conducted in 1905 and figures for 1914 were calculated based on the number of registered births and deaths in the intervening period. Conducting a census in the early twentieth century was a mammoth task, involving manually recording individuals, and therefore the resulting figures are widely disputed. Officially, the population of the empire totalled 18.5 million people. There were over

Henry Morgenthau, pictured in 1913.

15 million Muslims, 1.7 million Greek Orthodox and 1.2 million Armenians, divided into Armenian Orthodox and Armenian Catholics, as well as around 200,000 Jews and 65,000 Protestants of various denominations. Most of the figures were underestimations. The Armenian Patriarchate, the official body of the Armenian Church, assessed the number of Armenians in the Ottoman Empire at 2.1 million in 1912.

Henry Morgenthau began ambassadorial life largely removed from the complications of the country in which he lived. The American Embassy was a three-storey marble building with walled gardens that looked down on the steadily flowing waterway of the Golden Horn, along which the steamers chugged their way to and from the Bosphorus. In his early days, as Morgenthau walked the corridors, he found himself humming the refrain, "I dreamt I dwelt in marble halls". He immersed himself in the diplomatic set in Constantinople, trying to gain insight into the world of statecraft from career diplomats at "a continuous succession of luncheons, teas, dinners and formal state functions". It was a lavish and cordial baptism of fire.

The US Embassy in Constantinople.

The government to which Morgenthau represented American interests was technically a constitutional monarchy. Half a decade before, a Turkish nationalist uprising, supported by much of the military, had forced the Sultan to reinstate the constitution and restore the country's parliament. In the process of the Young Turk revolution, Sultan Abdul Hamid was deposed and replaced by his more compliant brother, Mohammed V. While the new Sultan occupied himself with the worldly trappings of royalty, the empire was run by the Committee of Union and Progress (CUP), the party with control of government. Two men predominantly held the levers of power in 1914: Mehmed Talaat, the Minister of the Interior and Ismail Enver, the Minister of War.

Talaat's broad shoulders, which had once carried rail passengers' luggage in a past life, gave the Ottoman Empire's Minister of the Interior considerable presence; Morgenthau described him as "a great hulk of a man". Talaat was determined, shrewd and held a long-fostered hatred of Armenians. In a casual conversation at a business meeting with a Danish university professor in 1910, the then rising star of the Young Turk movement had told his listener, "You see, between us [the Turks] and this people there is an incompatibility which cannot be solved in a peaceful manner; either they will completely undermine us, or we will have to annihilate them. If I ever come to power in this country, I will use all my might to exterminate the Armenians." Along with Greeks, Armenians accounted for a comparatively large element of Ottoman-Turkey's middle class, although the vast majority—estimated to be as high as eighty percent—were in fact peasants. In many cities there were Armenian businesses owners, merchants, bankers and lawyers—as non-Turks they were banned from holding many positions in high office—and they were often viewed with suspicion because of their wealth, religion and ethnicity. If Morgenthau picked up on Talaat's hatred of Armenians, it was not a fact that he mentioned in his early letters home. In late January 1914, Morgenthau's wife, Josephine, came to join him in Constantinople. Morgenthau had by this time developed good relations with Talaat and the American ambassador inquired of the Minister if he could help him arrange to meet his wife at the border town of Adrianople, where her train would enter Turkey. Talaat was astounded and replied "What! Going to all this trouble to meet one's wife. I never heard of such a thing … In Turkey we let our wives come to us, we do not go to them." In the event, Talaat acquiesced and arranged for Morgenthau to be entertained by the governor in Adrianople.

Talaat's right-hand men shared the goal of the Young Turk leadership to 'Turkify' the empire. In short, they despised the non-Turk elements in society, which included

SS *George Washington.*

Greeks, Assyrians and Armenians. As well as animosity rooted in the elevated social position held by some members of minorities, there was a second, arguably equally significant force behind the hatred of Armenians: their longstanding connection with Russia. The Ottoman Empire had been to war with Russia on multiple occasions. In the Crimean War in the 1850s, Britain and France had come to Turkey's aid to stop Russian expansion, but by 1877 Turkey and Russia were again at war. This time the Ottomans were routed and the Russian advance was only halted when Britain threatened to intervene. Armenians living in the Ottoman Empire's eastern provinces which had fallen to the Russians had welcomed the invaders with open arms. They had endured attacks from Kurdish Muslim armed groups and the arrival of Christian Russians provided welcome relief. The post-war Treaty of Berlin required the Ottoman government "to carry out without further delay the improvements and reforms demanded ... in the provinces inhabited by the Armenians, and to guarantee their security". The reverse happened. Armenian opposition to Kurdish attacks was brutally put down in 1894; Ottoman soldiers burned Armenian villages and it was claimed the Armenians were "in general revolt with the aim of striking at Islam". In 1895, a wave of violence broke out, which culminated in nearly 3,000 Armenians being burned alive in a cathedral in Urfa in southeast Turkey.

The Young Turk revolution did not signal the end of the attacks. In April 1909, as loyalists to Abdul Hamid attempted to oust the new Young Turk administration in Constantinople and restore the former sultan to the throne, rumours circulated in Adana that the Armenians were planning an armed uprising. The Armenian quarter was attacked by a Muslim mob. The violence spread to the surrounding region. In a few towns, Armenians succeeded in defending themselves, but in many places the mobs were supported by government troops who had been sent to quell the violence. More than 30,000 Armenians were slaughtered in the district of Adana and over 4,000 Armenian homes were torched in Adana city itself. *The New York Times* published an eyewitness testimony from an American missionary: "Adana is in a pitiable condition. The town has been pillaged and destroyed ... It is impossible to estimate the number killed. The corpses lie scattered throughout the streets."

The death toll was so great that Turkey's new government announced a formal investigation. Officials admitted that there had been no planned uprising by Armenians, but disputed the death toll; it was initially claimed that only 1,500 non-Muslims and 1,900 Muslims had been killed. One member of parliament who was part of the commission investigating the Adana massacres was Hagop Babikian. In an interview with a journalist he admitted the direct involvement of local authorities in inciting the violence. "The former mufti of Bagce began going here and there and saying that freedom and the Constitution were inventions of the Christians, who are opposed to the sharia [Islamic law]; in this fashion, he began to stir up the population and turn them against the Christians." Babikian also told reporters, "The national government did not take part in them [the massacres] but was the reason for them. The local authorities, for their part, were implicated in them." He also admitted that official documents proved the Armenians had not caused the 'disorders'. Details of the higher death toll reported in the European press were, he said, "by no means exaggerated and even fell short of the truth". Babikian's report for the Commission was left in a drawer for three years and his reputation publicly discredited. When Morgenthau visited Adana on his way back to Constantinople after a tour of Palestine in spring 1914, he wrote in his diary: "Heard all about the massacre. It must have been fierce. They all claim it was incited or at any rate encouraged by government officials and could have been stopped. Feeling between Armenians and Moslems is still terrible. You can see and feel the hatred."

Armenian women, as depicted in the late 19th century.

Talaat and his co-leaders of the CUP assumed that the Armenians not only fostered nationalist ambitions—a not entirely inaccurate assessment as there had been several historical Armenian nationalist movements—but also that they represented a fifth column within the population. The violence against the Armenians in 1895 had been partially stayed by strong objections from Great Britain, France and Russia, objections which only served to confirm that suspicion. For years, the Ottoman Empire had been in decline and had steadily lost territory. The failure of previous governments to deal with the Christian 'menace', and the resultant meddling interference from Christian nations, seemingly "explained all the woes from which Turkey had suffered in modern times". At the start of 1914, the United States' ambassador to Ottoman-Turkey had almost nothing to do with the Armenians, but all that was to change with the coming of the Great War.

2. THE DRUMS OF WAR

From the picturesque surrounds of Morgenthau's residence, war seemed but a distant prospect. He wrote in his diary on Sunday 7 June 1914, "I got up early and sat on the porch overlooking the Bosporus ... It was an inspiring sight to see the little steamboats plying up the river, sail boats floating along, and some tugs dragging lots of small fishing boats etc. up against the tide ... I felt as though I was on a boat, for, unless one looks straight down, you can not see the street but only the water." But the peace was about to be torn apart. A few weeks later, Archduke Franz Ferdinand of Austria, along with his wife, was assassinated as his car drove through the streets of Sarajevo.

On 4 July, a requiem mass for the murdered duke and duchess was held at a church on the Grand Rue de Pera, now known as Istiklal Caddessi, the most visited street in

The German Ambassador to the Ottoman Empire, Baron von Wangenheim.

modern-day Istanbul (Constantinople). The service was "dignified and beautiful" and at the end, each of the Constantinople diplomats shook hands with the Austrian ambassador, before getting into their cars to be driven to the American Embassy. There, the mourning atmosphere evaporated as Constantinople's great and good celebrated American Independence Day. The party went on into the night, the gardens of the Embassy lit by Chinese lanterns and exploding fireworks. One notable diplomat was absent however: the German ambassador, Baron von Wangenheim.

Wangenheim was no stranger to Constantinople: he had spent five years as First Secretary to the German Embassy from 1899 to 1904, returning as full ambassador in 1912. A son of German nobility, he had complete disdain for those beneath him, maintaining a bristling sense of Prussian superiority; he once told Morgenthau, "we keep the [German] governing classes pure, unmixed of blood." But he was also capable of restraint. Morgenthau, while personally disliking him, could only marvel, as "he had precisely that combination of force, persuasiveness and brutality which was needed in dealing with the Turkish character". Wangenheim's passport photograph from the time shows a face with dark, brooding eyes and a firm jaw. He was not a man destined to be very sympathetic to the plight of the Armenians. Wangenheim was absent from the festivities because he had been called back to Berlin, to sit on the Kaiser's Imperial Council, at which the Kaiser reportedly looked each of his General Staff in the eye and asked them if they were ready for war. To a man, they replied yes. On 27 July, Morgenthau attended a gathering at the Italian Embassy, where diplomats and their wives from the nations which were about to begin slaughtering one another ate, drank and danced together. Morgenthau wrote in his diary that night, "All talked of war." He later recalled, "everyone seemed to realize that this peaceful, frivolous life was transitory, and that at any moment might come the spark that was to set everything aflame." The following day, Austria-Hungary declared war on Serbia. Within a week, the whole of Europe was plunged into what would turn out to be the deadliest conflict humanity had ever witnessed.

Even though Turkey was officially neutral, from the start of August, preparations for war continued apace. Banking restrictions were imposed and hotels began to make foreigners pay in cash for their rooms each night. Unknown to almost every-one outside of the CUP leadership and the German Imperial Council, Germany and Turkey had already signed a secret pact, which would bring Turkey into the war on the side of Germany and Austria-Hungary, although it was already patently clear where the Turkish sympathies lay. In late August, the government introduced conscription for all males between the ages of eighteen and forty-five. On 19 August, Morgenthau's chauffeur was called up: "My chaffeur [sic] told me of his call for military service. He has a wife and three children whom he would leave penniless. The hardships of mobilization are heartrending. It is terrible to see those poor recruits marching through the city." Very few citizens wanted to be conscripted, as they often received little food and were very poorly equipped. In the far eastern *vilayet* of Van, which was majority Armenian, the authorities took a typically heavy-handed approach to secure men to fight. On Sunday 9 August, soldiers arrived outside the city's cathedral. As the congregation filed out of the service, all the men were detained and marched to the city barracks. The army then began requisitioning animals and carts in villages and drafting peasants. The combination of both actions instantly removed most of the labourers and farm animals from the fields at the height of the harvest and the price of bread soared. Among those drafted into uniform in autumn 1914 were an estimated 60,000 Armenians. In one fell swoop, the Armenian community had been denuded of the majority of those capable of defending it.

Many in the Armenian community were already suffering by early summer 1914. For years, the CUP had actively encouraged Muslim Turks to avoid patronizing Christian-owned shops, but from February 1914 onwards this had become a concerted campaign. Pamphlets were produced to inspire Turks to forgo purchasing from 'foreign' businesses. One pamphlet, entitled 'A Way of Liberation for Muslims', read: "how we are going to celebrate the day on which Turks and Muslims buy things from each other only ... we are not asking for a great sacrifice from you in order to reach that day ... In the beginning this might seem difficult. However, we shall eventually get used to it." Supported by guild organizations and localized trading networks, the boycott was not just a series of isolated acts of prejudice, but a nationwide movement. Morgenthau wrote that it illustrated "the topsy-turvy national organization of Turkey, for here we had a nation engaging in a commercial boycott against its own subjects". Armenian and Greek peasants were prevented from delivering their goods to market and non-Muslim shops, with the exception of Jewish businesses, were shunned.

Turkish soldiers in Constantinople at the declaration of war.

The economic impact of the boycott was devastating; in the province of Izmir production of grains, fruit, cotton, sugar and tobacco all fell, some by as much as forty percent in a single year (1914). But the campaign achieved its objective. Over time, the boycott ruined hundreds of Armenian and Greek tradesmen.

As in many towns, the Armenian merchants in Diyarbakir played a key role in regional economy. The city, nestled on the banks of the Tigris, had become the centre of a booming textile industry since the late nineteenth century, exporting silk and cotton; Diyarbakir handkerchiefs and sheets were famed across the region. In the whole province, which shared its name with its largest city, there were around 100,000 Armenians, as well as Assyrian and other Christians. Diyarbekir had been scarred by the violence of 1895—more than a thousand Armenians had been killed in the city—but although Christian Armenians were intensely disliked, many had returned to their homes and had been permitted to get on with their lives. On 18 August 1914, the fragile truce was shattered. A Muslim mob, reportedly encouraged by the local police chief, set fire to parts of the central market and began looting and burning Christians' shops. Some of the mob claimed to be collecting 'contributions' to the war effort. The authorities stood by and watched. It was a harbinger of what was to come.

Turkish neutrality lasted only until the autumn, when the Ottoman Navy launched a surprise attack on the Russian Black Sea port of Odessa. In the first week of November, Russia officially declared war, making Ottoman-Turkey an enemy of Britain and France, triggering a mass exodus of foreign nationals. Morgenthau, as an American, was permitted to stay. The American ambassador found himself the surprise custodian of valuables for a range of foreign evacuees, who felt they could rely on the United States' neutrality and the sturdiness of the U.S. Embassy's safe; a journalist for *The Times* even inquired of Morgenthau if he could leave his butterfly collection for safekeeping. Morgenthau did accept the request to look after what was left of the British ambassador's official archive; the American ambassador had sat with his British counterpart and watched as he calmly cast page after page of documents into a roaring fire at his embassy, papers which "contained the embassy records for probably a hundred years".

With Russia now formally an enemy, attention was already beginning to turn to the Armenians. The police department in Constantinople had previously collected the names, addresses and photographs of around 2,000 Armenian 'notables': doctors, professors, political agitators and men of high standing. But it was not just notables who were causing concern. The old fear of the fifth column was once again front and centre.

In 1914, the Armenian population was concentrated in what is now eastern Turkey. Large parts of the rural population around towns such as Erzerum, and Harput were Armenian and there had been plans—forced upon the Ottomans by European powers in a treaty in 1878 after Russia defeated Turkey in a war—to grant eastern Armenians a level of autonomy. Although the vast majority of Armenians had no connection with Russia, past history implied that the Armenians were in the Russian camp. Their position was not aided by the fact that the Russian Tsar had personally appealed to the Armenians to rise up in support of Russia in the war, a written invitation the CUP-controlled newspaper, *Tanin*, gleefully published in October 1914. In some areas, the local authorities were not waiting for any new evidence of Armenian disloyalty. In the Armenian town of Zeitun in central Turkey, the entire Armenian population was ordered to hand in their weapons, down to the very last knife.

Despite the history of past massacres, most Armenians identified far more with Turkey than with Russia. The 10 November circular from the Patriarchate—the head of the Armenian church—asserted that Armenians throughout the provinces had "obeyed the mobilization order by answering the call ... to serve in the armed forces, complying with the war requisitions ... and gladly responding to the appeal for funds ... the Armenian nation, as an indivisible part of the Ottoman fatherland, is, as the occasion demands, prepared to make every sacrifice to demonstrate its loyalty and patriotism". In one town, an Armenian-run school even set up an accelerated programme to train Armenian nurses to treat wounded Turkish soldiers. In truth, no effort on the part of Armenian communities, or their representatives, would prove sufficient: it had been decided long before by Talaat and his co-leaders that the Armenians' guilt was an original sin for which they could never atone.

Other preparations were also underway. From September 1914 onwards, the CUP began expanding party 'Special Organizations'. The organizations were effectively party militia but almost no documents of their activities prior to autumn 1914 survive. Suddenly, recruitment boomed. On the orders of party leadership, criminals were released from prisons and dispatched to the eastern provinces. The two largest bands concentrated in Erzerum and Trebizond, where they immediately began a campaign of violence and looting. Although one local party organization informed the central committee it had "struggled to find sufficient numbers of people who are frequently engaged in murder and theft", by the end of the autumn 1914, an estimated 10,000 convicts had been enrolled into '*chetes*'. They were to become the

Armenian women in Borjomi,
Georgia, 1912.

Turkish government's killing squads. Meanwhile, conscripted soldiers who had
been ordered east, but who had no barracks to sleep in, had evicted some Armenian
villages wholesale and requisitioned their houses and food.

On 5 December 1914, the German consul in Erzerum, Joseph Schwarz, telegrammed his boss, Wangenheim. "The Armenian population of the Vilayet of
Erzerum, especially the country people, is very worried because of a few incidents
which they see as harbingers of new massacres." He reported that Turkish irregulars, the *chetes*, had abducted and then murdered a priest with a shotgun and in
another village men had been taken prisoner and held in chains by soldiers until
villagers paid a ransom. "It is a matter of fact that Turkish officers do not see eye to
eye with the Armenians and reproach them with being friendly to Russia ... the old
hatred is rising again."

3. SCAPEGOATS

The Turkish intent had always been to attack Russia but Ottoman forces had already found themselves engaged with the British in Persia (Iran) in early November, when Britain moved to secure its Persian oilfields. In late 1914 however, the British and French were preoccupied with halting the German advance into Belgium at Ypres.

Turkey's eastern border with the Caucasus was its most exposed and Russian forces were already massing within striking distance of areas with significant Armenian populations. Turkish irregulars began probing attacks, followed by a full offensive by the Turkish Third Army—the headquarters of which was in Erzerum—in late December. Enver had travelled from Constantinople to take personal command of the attack. Most of the Turkish soldiers were completely unequipped to fight 5,000 feet above sea level; one Turkish official told Morgenthau on 14 December that they were "dying like flies, being unaccustomed to the cold weather". Worse was to come. The Ottoman offensive began on 22 December and quickly ran into difficulty. Artillery support was left behind because of deep snow and the men marched through the drifts overnight in temperatures well below freezing. Soldiers lost each other in the pine forests amidst the swirling snow flurries and what had meant to be a coordinated attack on Sarikamish became a disjointed advance, in which single regiments were mown down one by one by Russian gunners. Within in days, most of the Turkish Third Army was surrounded and Enver scuttled back to Erzerum. Out of the nearly 100,000 soldiers who began the attack, more than 80,000 were killed or taken prisoner. A German officer attached to Enver's general staff described the battle as "a disaster which for rapidity and completeness is without parallel in military history". Luckily for the Turks, the Russian force opposing them, which had initially comprised over 100,000 men had been depleted to around 60,000 so the Russians could reinforce their western front. As a result, after soundly beating the Enver's Third Army, they withdrew again, as they were tasked only with defending the Caucasus border.

A scapegoat for the humiliating defeat was quickly found. As Armenian soldiers had been seen deserting from the Third Army—among many other non-Armenians who did not fancy their chances on the snowy slopes—and because there were two volunteer Armenian brigades among the defending Russians, it was immediately claimed that the cause of the defeat was an Armenian plot. The defeat of the Turkish army has been credited as the trigger of *chete* attacks on Armenian villages along the frontier, but in actual fact, attacks on the Armenian population began even before Enver had assumed command. *Chete* bands started attacking villages around Erzerum and as far south as Van, slaughtering men and sometimes women and children.

The *chetes* around Van were drawn from the Kurdish population and were recruited with an offer of an amnesty for all past crimes, which they gladly accepted as a license to commit new ones. The Kurds, along with another ethnic group, Circassians, had a historically less than cordial relationship with Armenians. In Van, Kurdish groups in the region were effectively autonomous, but were brought into line by the authorities' use of bribes. Occasionally they would raid villages, often Armenian ones, to acquire food, animals and women. By December 1914, Kurdish *chetes* were being employed to do just that. On 15 December, the member of the Ottoman Parliament for Van province, Arshag Vramian, wrote a letter of complaint to Talaat, outlining the violence that had occurred in the region. He recounted the specific devastation caused to the village of Hazaren: "More than five thousand animals, grain and all the farm implements were taken and the village church was demolished." He added that "similar scenes are being repeated everywhere; well organized massacres and looting, razed villages". In a bold statement, that implies he was already aware that the Armenian community were likely to be targeted during the war, he asserted to the Minister of the Interior, "An anti-Christian policy will not help save the country ... The government must cease to consider the Armenian elements in the empire as enemies." His pleas fell on deaf ears.

Sometime in December 1914 or January 1915, Talaat is said to have held a series of meetings with senior members of the CUP. A handwritten account of one meeting lays out a plan to systematically eradicate the Armenian population. Step by step, it outlines the approach to be used. First, known anti-government figures are to be arrested, then any weapons owned by Armenians confiscated. Next, the document suggests encouraging massacres by local Muslims, "exterminating" all males under fifty years of age and "carrying away" families. The army are responsible for "killing off" all Armenians in uniform. The penultimate line states, "All action to begin every-where simultaneously, and thus leave no time for preparation of defensive measures."

In all likelihood, the documents, obtained by the British through an informant, are sophisticated fakes, although the British believed them to be genuine when they surfaced in 1916. In one sense, while much academic research time has been spent examining their authenticity, it does not matter. What is startling about what was done to Armenians across the Ottoman Empire in 1915 is that it followed precisely that pattern and began simultaneously. From the moment the Armenian genocide got underway, it was clearly planned and orchestrated.

Kurdish cavalry.

On Sunday 21 March 1915, Morgenthau noted in his diary, "The authorities [in Trebizond] have forced all Armenians and Greeks liable to military service to make roads and hew stones, [they] may not carry arms." From March onwards, the few Armenian soldiers who had received weapons had them taken off them. A rumour was spread that Armenian soldiers had turned their rifles on their Turkish superiors at Sarikamish—so well spread in fact that Wangenheim even telegrammed Berlin attesting to the false fact. In reality, Armenians were almost always used behind the front; even the German Embassy's in-house Armenian expert during the war admitted the notion they had turned their guns on men in the same uniform was "out of the question". The labour battalions, typically given the task of road-building, were systemically exterminated. A German nurse working in Mesereh recounted: "Crowds of young Armenians, who had been conscripted as soldiers to build roads were taken to Mesereh ... several days later they were led away by armed soldiers—1,200 men in total. It was said that they were to build roads again. Apparently they did work for several days ... then they were led further on to Diyarbakir bound together ... and killed."

Deyarbekir itself was in a fit of war hysteria. The rule of law was hanging by a thread, soldiers were deserting in droves and the population was nervous; it was rumoured in the bazaars that Constantinople had been taken by the Russians, a rumour surprisingly hard to disprove as Constantinople was nearly 800 miles away to the west and news in wartime travelled with all the speed and accuracy of Chinese whispers. In March, the *vilayet* of Deyarbekir was given a new governor.

Dr Mehmed Resid had been one of the founders of the CUP. Born in the Caucasus, his family had immigrated to Russia and he had subsequently trained in military medicine. After the Young Turk revolution, he left the military and entered politics. His appearance was that of a typical Turkish authority figure: an impressively coiffured moustache, topped by pince-nez and a fez. The previous governor of the region had been relatively tolerant of Armenians, but Resid had other plans. Shortly after arrival at his new post he organized a "Committee of Enquiry" to provide "a solution of the Armenian question". He would later justify what followed in chillingly scientific terms: "Either the Armenians would eliminate the Turks or the Turks would eliminate the Armenians. I didn't hesitate for one moment when confronted with this dilemma. My Turkish identity won out over my profession. I thought: we must destroy them before they destroy us. If you ask me how I as a doctor could commit murder, my answer is simple: the Armenians had become dangerous microbes in the body of this country. And surely it is a doctor's duty to kill bacteria?"

The *chetes* in the province were expanded and a representative, reportedly sent by Resid himself, travelled around to Kurdish villages encouraging action against the 'infidels'. The religious element was central to much of the Turkish anti-Christian and Armenian discourse. One popular quasi-prayer recited was, "God, make their children orphans, make widows of their wives ... and give their property to Muslims." The entire conflict was presented by the CUP as inherently religious in character. Shortly after the official declaration of war in November 1914, the Ottoman religious leader declared the war was a *jihad*—a holy war—in which it was "a religious duty for all the Muslims in all countries, whether young or old, infantry or cavalry, to resort to *jihad* with all their properties and lives". The Armenians were not just viewed as enemies of the Turkish Muslim identity, they were viewed as enemies of God.

Militia were being organized around the country. In Harput, where the four central towns had a slim majority of Armenians, anti-Armenian propaganda was spreading like wild fire. Stories circulated that following the defeat of the Third Army, the Muslim population in the eastern border regions had been subject to terrible atrocities by Russian and Armenian soldiers. They were fake, but the local authorities were already pressing ahead with organizing *chetes*. That month, the governor of the Harput *vilayet* told a German diplomat passing through the region that the Armenians in Turkey were going to be "exterminated" because they "had grown in wealth and numbers, until they had become a menace to the Turkish race".

4. REVOLT AND RESISTANCE

Apologists for the treatment of the Armenians in the Ottoman Empire in the First World War consistently point to two examples where Armenians apparently confirmed Turkish fears. At Zeitun and Van in early 1915 Armenians rebelled, in one case with the direct assistance of Russia.

Zeitun's residents had proved stubbornly independent over the previous century. Until 1862 the region had been autonomous, albeit paying for its autonomy with an annual tribute to the Sultan, and in the massacres of 1895, the city successfully repelled all attacks. Situated in a valley at the foot of a mountain, Zeitun and its surrounding six villages were home to an almost exclusively Armenian population of 22,000 in 1914. All the young men were mobilized in August when conscription was introduced, after which local gendarmes began harassing residents, forcing their way into homes, openly stealing, and mistreating and occasionally raping women. Not all of those drafted into uniform stayed and around a hundred Armenian deserters ran away and hid among the mountains. On 8 March, a group of deserters killed twelve Turkish soldiers, before returning to their hideout in a monastery. Residents of Zeitun immediately sent representatives to the group to call on them to halt any further attacks. Ten days later, 5,000 Turkish soldiers, with supporting artillery, arrived from Aleppo. A few days later all the government officials disappeared from the city. When the army moved to attack the monastery, the advancing soldiers discovered the deserters had fled. Instead of returning to Aleppo the three regiments surrounded Zeitun.

On 30 March, Morgenthau met Talaat who gave him what he claimed were the "full details" of events at Zeitun. The conflict

was caused by some Armenian deserters attempting to rescue some of their colleagues who were in prison ... They fled to their cloister where the gendarmes are now pursuing them". Morgenthau had also been updated by the American consul in Aleppo, and the ambassador deemed the situation serious enough to cable Washington: "Have received several disquieting reports from [the] Consul [in] Aleppo regarding troubles between Turkish troops and Armenians at Zeitoun [sic] ... Serious friction has occurred between Turkish troops and Armenian deserters ... but [the] Government claims there is no fear of trouble spreading to surrounding districts.

The government had a clear solution to preventing the trouble spreading: the entire population of Zeitun was to be deported.

The army entered the city on 8 April 1915 and, beginning with leading citizens and their families, forced the Armenians onto the road. When ordered to present themselves at the military barracks, a foreigner living in one of the nearby towns reported, "They obeyed the summons without the least suspicion, believing themselves to be on excellent terms with the authorities. Some of them took a little money, others some clothing or wraps, but the majority came in their working clothes and brought nothing with them ... They were ordered to leave the town at once without returning to their homes." A few managed to bring blankets and donkeys, but most found themselves on the road in nothing but the clothes on their back. The Armenian patriarch recorded, "Thus, [a] total of around 18,000 people was put on the road in three days; nearly 6,000 were set marching in the direction of Konya [Konia] and Eregli ... 5,000 more were sent towards Aleppo." The premeditation of the deportations is clear. As the Armenians were force-marched out of Zeitun, Muslim refugees—made homeless following the Ottoman Empire's defeat in the

Armenian refugees on the road. Location unknown.

1912-13 Balkan War—were moved into their houses; previously the refugees had lived in camps paid for by the government. One young Armenian girl who was one of the few survivors, remembered seeing the new occupants of the villages chopping down the fruit trees for firewood. Most of the exiles travelled on foot, those that had livestock typically had it stolen. One eyewitness recalled, "I came across another characteristic case. A citizen of Zeitoun [sic], formerly a rich man, leading two donkeys, the last remnants of his fortune. A gendarme [a catch-all term used to describe Turkish soldiers and *chetes*] who came along and seized their bridles; the Armenian implored him to leave them, saying that he was on the verge of starvation. The only answer he received from the Turk was a shower of blows, repeated until he rolled over in the dust; even then the Turk continued landing blows on him, till the dust was turned into blood-soaked mud; then he gave a final kick and went off with the donkeys." The Turks escorting the ragged convoy made the Armenians sleep in the open and prevented people in the towns and villages they passed through from giving them food and clothing. The residents of Zeitun had the dubious distinction of being the first Armenians to be deported and marched to death.

The uprising in Van took place after the deportation of Zeitun, news of which had reached the Armenians in Van. In the words of an American missionary who later watched the drama unfold, "Van was one of the most beautiful cities in Asiatic Turkey—a city of gardens and vineyards, situated on Lake Van in the centre of a plateau bordered by magnificent mountains." On 17 April, *chetes* were stationed in a barracks in the Armenian quarter of the city, which had previously been left unmanned, and the following day massacres began in the Armenian villages around Van. A Venezuelan mercenary, serving as an officer in the Ottoman Army, tried to intervene to stop the murderous rampage by Turks and Kurds—many of whom were neighbours of the town's Armenians—in Aldicevaz on 20 April. He ordered the mayor, who was leading a mob, to desist. The mayor replied he had been given an "unequivocal order emanating from the governor-general of the province to exterminate all Armenian males of twelve years of age and over".

The residents of Van itself determined not to be taken by surprise. On 20 April thousands barricaded themselves into the old quarter. Those that did not were quickly slaughtered by Kurdish *chetes*; dogs fought over the bodies until gathered by the authorities and burned. Some Armenians managed to take refuge in an American missionary hospital in the town; it was soon treating triple its capacity of fifty patients and the missionary compound and church were crammed with desperate families. One missionary recalled seeing one woman "whose husband was serving in

Armenians defending the walls of Van in the spring of 1915.

the Turkish army and whose twelve-year-old boy was slain before her eyes. She was wounded herself, as well as her two remaining children, one four years and the other eleven months old. I shall never forget the drooping look of the little one and the wounded arm that hung by his side, nor the woman herself, who was almost mad".

With limited weapons, but making full use of the familiar urban environment, the Armenians in the old quarter held off their attackers on the first day and through the night, as the fires from the torched surrounding villages turned the skyline blood red. The following day, the population of Constantinople woke to find the front pages of the newspapers informing them of an "Armenian revolt" in Van. The *chetes* were joined by regular Turkish forces, who bombarded the old city with artillery, deliberately targeting a historic cathedral. But the resistance still clung on, improvising a cartridge factory to replenish their ammunition, organizing the rationing of food and dispatching secret messengers in the hope of receiving assistance from the Russians. Even children helped, one later remembering, "We children used to go from house to house to gather brass candle bars to make shells for the bullets. They even learned to make the powder ... Sometimes the fighting was at very close range, from one house to another." As the attempted massacre became a siege, Armenian Russian volunteers and a brigade of Cossack cavalry were given orders to advance south from Yerevan towards Van. The Ottoman units supposedly guarding the northern frontier of Van province crumbled and fled. On 19 May, the Turks withdrew, leaving the city under Armenian control as Russian cavalry bore down on Van. The Armenians emerged from behind the barricades to find their liberators in sight. A western missionary recorded, "The joy of the people was boundless; tears of gladness and emotion for what they had suffered during the past month rolled down their cheeks as they made them [the Russians] welcome." There are several recorded instances of Armenians murdering wounded Turkish soldiers in cold blood, but generally the victorious Armenians demonstrated incredible restraint. The Turks had left behind their wounded in one hospital; a missionary later wrote how Armenian fighters helped care for them, something he doubted even "European soldiers" would have done.

The siege of Van had lasted just over a month. Nearly miraculously, 30,000 Armenian residents of Van and an estimated 15,000 refugees had survived, living together in a built-up area of less than a few square miles. Around 1,500 armed Armenians had beaten off 5,000 Turkish soldiers and *chetes*. Van was dressed up as the fulfilment of the Turkish government's worst nightmare: a revolt of Armenians in Turkey, supported by Russia. Morgenthau had little time for the Turkish narrative: "After massacring hundreds of thousands of Armenians in the course of thirty years, outraging their women and girls, and robbing and maltreating them in every conceivable way, the Turks still apparently believed they had the right to expect from them the most enthusiastic 'loyalty'." It was claimed that the Armenians had killed Turks fleeing the Russian advance: Enver stated 120,000 had been slaughtered, a problematic figure, given that there were only 30,000 Turks recorded as living in the entire province. In reality, as Talaat admitted to the German Embassy at the time, 400 Armenian fighters had been killed and several hundred Turkish troops. The Russians collected over 55,000 bodies from the area around Van; the actual death toll of Armenian civilians was probably far higher. Among the many murdered was the Van member of parliament, Arshag Vramian, who had written to Talaat only a few months before, imploring him to stop viewing the Armenians as enemies of the Ottoman Empire.

An Armenian peasant in his eighties, fleeing his home in a village north of Lake Van along a muddy road towards the areas under Russian control, had already grasped the scale of events. He told a passing western diplomat, "I have seen the ravages of the Crimean War, the Russo-Turkish war of 1877–78, the Armenian massacres of 1894–96, and the reign of terror which then followed until the year 1914; but the massacres which have been going on since April of the current year are simply appalling, and by far the most terrible blow which the Armenian nation has been subject to throughout the course of its long history."

5. A GENOCIDE BEGINS

Although the Armenians desperately defending themselves in Van were unaware of it, beyond the barricades a genocide was underway. Starting on the night of 24 April 1915, a wave of coordinated arrests took place in Constantinople. The editors of an Armenian newspaper were detained, along with over 200 other prominent Armenians who had made the previously compiled lists, which included doctors, writers, teachers and merchants. Initially they were held by police and then transported by train to Ayandjik, around twelve miles west of Constantinople; they were made to buy their own tickets at the railway station. It was a beginning of a journey that would take them along the Turkish government's newly organized deportation route from one corner of Turkey to the other; almost all of them would die before they reached their intended destination.

Armenians being publicly executed in Constantinople, June 1915.

In Diyabekir, the new governor, Mehmet Resid, in his exceptional keenness to proceed with eliminating the Armenians, had arrested local religious leaders five days earlier and almost all the Armenian politicians in Diyarbakir on the 21st. In Harput the first arrests of leaders took place on 4 April, while arrests in many other provinces occurred over the following weeks. Around 200 Armenians were detained in Erzerum on the night of 24 April and crammed together in squalid cells.

The very evening that police across Constantinople were banging down doors and arresting en masse the Armenian elite of the city, Talaat joined Morgenthau and his wife for dinner. The other guests were the Chief Rabbi, Chaim Nahoum, and his wife, and Morgenthau's interpreter and legal counsel on the Embassy staff, a Turkish-Armenian called Arshag Shmavonian. After the meal, Morgenthau's wife, Josephine, and the wife of the Chief Rabbi left to go to the cinema while the men talked shop. The Minister of the Interior was frank with his host, explaining that any attempts at revolution during the war would be crushed. When quizzed about the Armenians he admitted that the government had arrested a "great many" of them, but claimed they planned "to put them among the Turks in the interior where they can do no harm".

On 26 April, the Treasurer of the American Board of Commissioners for Foreign Mission in Constantinople—effectively the chief representative of the numerous American missionaries in the country—called on Morgenthau. William Peet was accompanied by another American missionary, Doctor Caleb Gates, who was president of a pioneer international school in Constantinople—Robert College—which still exists today. Both men had spent years in Turkey and were anything but starry-eyed religious zealots. When Enver paid a formal visit to Robert College at the request of Morgenthau before the war, he was deeply impressed. He told Morgenthau, "I expected to find these missionaries as they are pictured in the Berlin newspapers, with long hair and hanging jaws, and hands clasped constantly in a prayerful attitude. But here is Dr. Gates, talking Turkish like a native and acting like a man of the world. I am more than pleased. Thank you for bringing me." Both Peet and Gates maintained good contacts with other missionaries in Turkey. They presented Morgenthau with "very disquieting news" of events in Zeitun and Van. The next day, Morgenthau sent a confidential cable to the Secretary of State in Washington: "Over [a] hundred Armenians of better class were arrested ostensibly to prevent revolutionary propaganda ... Have also received unfavourable reports about Armenians in interior provinces."

Morgenthau was not the only diplomat badgering the Secretary of State. The Russian ambassador in Washington had also been making an impression.

The Secretary replied to Morgenthau later that day: "You will please bring the matter to the attention of the [Turkish] government, urging upon it the use of effective means for the protection of Armenians from violence at the hands of those of other religions." Colonel Leipzig, the German military attaché in Constantinople, who was a close friend of Wangeheim's, explained to Morgenthau the official reasoning for the arrests, which the ambassador recorded in his diary entry for the day: "[Col. Leipzig] told me that Armenians, incited by the Russians, had been in possession of Van for 12 days, and that 400 of them were killed there ... they felt alarmed lest they would do similar things in Constantinople and therefore they concluded to send all prominent Armenians to Ayandjik [near Angora], where they would be prevented from doing any harm." Already, even though the siege of Van was not yet over, it had become the case for the prosecution against the Armenians. Morgenthau, in what would become a familiar pattern, sent another update about the treatment of Armenians to the Secretary of State three days later: "Continued reports of persecutions, plunder and massacres of Armenians in certain parts of empire had been received. Strong representations were made by Armenian Patriarch, Italian Ambassador, Bulgarian [Ambassador] and myself. Minister of War [Enver], to justify movement against Armenians, stated to me that Russian Armenians were responsible for destroying with bombs public buildings and post-office at Van ... As traveling in the eastern provinces has been stopped practically and all correspondence is under strict censorship it is impossible to know how true reports or statements are. From a report received today from consul at Aleppo it appears that the Turkish authorities are treating Armenian population of Zeitoun and Marash with incredible severity."

The American consul in Aleppo was Jesse Benjamin Jackson, a dapper forty-four-year-old former army sergeant and clerk in the House of Representatives who hailed from the Midwest. As Aleppo was to become the main staging post for eastward deportations, he was to have a front row seat to witness the suffering of hundreds of thousands of Armenians. Their plight would move him to organize a relief effort that would end up helping an estimated 150,000 refugees. His message to Morgenthau enclosed a report from a western missionary from Aintab, who had travelled to Aleppo to see Jackson specifically to report on what was happening. Jackson and the missionary had even persuaded the German Consulate to pass on the information (in code) to the German Embassy in the hope that they would also take action. Jackson added his own note: "In this way we hoped to be able to bring some pressure on the Ottoman Government to desist from the terrible measures that are being carried out ... [and] cause untold suffering to a helpless and innocent people."

Jesse B. Jackson, U.S. Consul in Aleppo.

Morgenthau was already too late to stop the deportations from Zeitun: by the time he was made aware of what had taken place by Jackson, the entire Armenian population had been uprooted and put on the road and their houses occupied by Turkish refugees. Marash was only around ten miles southeast of Zeitun and news of the actions by Armenian deserters did not take long to spread around the city. An American doctor who worked and taught at a hospital attached to a Christian college in Aintab, Fred Shepard, visited Marash in late March. He wrote to Jackson shortly afterwards. "I was in Marash for 48 hours from noon of Tuesday till noon of Thursday 18 March last week. There had no doubt been a plan to stir up a massacre at Marash over the Zeytun [sic] disturbances." Shepard claimed the immediate danger of massacre had been averted, but added that the imminent hostilities between the Armenians at Zeitun and the government would make it "somewhat difficult to control the Muslim mob at Marash".

Of the many Americans who stepped in to help Armenians during the genocide, Dr. Fred Shepard is perhaps one of the most revered. He was a modest man with sparkling eyes and bushy beard whose two loves in life were God and his patients. He travelled on horseback to distant villages to treat those who could not get to hospital and

Armenian women *fedayi* (militia), 1918.

was given a medal of merit by the Red Cross for his work caring for the Armenians following the 1909 massacre in Adana. At a special event held by the community in his honour, he told the adoring crown, "I did not come to this country to make money or to win a reputation. I came to bear witness to this, that God is Love. And if, by my work or my life, I have been able to show this to you, I have had my reward." As the genocide intensified in 1915 he would work tirelessly to help the emaciated, starving and diseased refugees. It would cost him his life.

The Armenians in Marash had already been forced to hand over their weapons, although the order had been used as an excuse to harass the Armenian population. Jackson's opposite number, the German consul in Aleppo, Walter Rössler, recorded in a memo, "the Armenian population also lost their weapons, mainly through preferred nightly house raids; soldiers beat Christians, women were molested under the pretext that they were going to be searched for weapons ... While the Armenians had to surrender their weapons, the Muslims had the opportunity to buy [gun] powder and small shot." A rumour spread around the town's Armenian population that the authorities had compiled a black list with the names of 600 notables. It was true. Within four weeks the Armenians in Marash would begin to follow in the footsteps of the residents of Zeitun.

6. ARREST AND TORTURE

News of events in Van had reached the outside world. On 26 April, *The New York Times*'s front page reported "Kurds massacre more Armenians", with the paper going on to describe a "great exodus". The article recounted in lurid detail the story of a young man named Hackatur, who managed to crawl out of a well which Kurdish *chetes* had filled with bodies. The headlines were dramatic, but there was no hint in the *Times* that the wave of violence was part of a more comprehensive programme of extermination underway across Turkey.

On 10 May, Morgenthau called on Talaat. The ambassador "found him in a bellicose humor ... I first spoke to him about a telegram I had received from the Department [of State] about Van, that Americans there were in danger. He telegraphed about it

The Ottoman Minister of the Interior and later Sultan, Mehmed Talaat.

in my presence ... I spoke to him about the Armenian refugees [from Zeitun, now] at Konia. He asked me: 'Are they Americans?' as much as to say: 'None of my business.' He said that they are not to be trusted and that it does not concern me. I told him ... I was a friend of the Armenians." The Minister of the Interior had the capacity to be extremely receptive to Morgenthau's concerns about American citizens—Talaat frequently dispatched cables immediately when Morgenthau presented him with such problems—but he was obdurate about the Armenians. Two days later, Jackson again got in touch with Morgenthau.

"Between 4,300 and 4,500 families, about 28,000 persons, are being removed by order of the Government from the districts of Zeitoun [sic] and Marash to distant places ... the sick drop by the wayside, women in critical condition giving birth to children that, according to reports, many mothers strangle or drown because of lack of means to fare for. Fathers exiled in one direction, mothers in another ... accompanying gendarmes are told they may do as they wish with the women and girls. The writer has personally seen several parties of the men that passed through Aleppo, and who were in a most deplorable plight, and wonders what must have been the condition of others that naturally were much less able to resist such treatment ... A traveller coming from Constantinople said that he met about 4,500 of these unfortunates on the way bound for Konia, and his description of their condition was appalling. The Armenians themselves say that they would by far have preferred a massacre, which would have been less disastrous for them."

The deportees from Zeitun who reached Konia were in a terrible state, as an American doctor at a Red Cross hospital there told Morgenthau in a letter in early May.

People have been brought here during the week past, several hundred every night, on the train ... That they were famishingly hungry and utterly wretched I have evidence both from my own eyesight, and testimony of others ... The crying of the children, the women almost falling and being pushed on by the guards, the scanty clothing, make a sight that one does not want to see again. The Turks in the market greeted them with 'Are these Giaours [infidels] dead yet' and other such remarks. A baby was born on the train last night, but the mother threw it out of the window that its sufferings might end at once.

There is no doubt that the order to the governors of the provinces to begin deporting Armenians came from Talaat, because one of the few governors who was reluctant took his objections straight to the Minister of the Interior. The governor of Erzerum, the Greek-born Hasan Tahsin, had already been transferred from Van in February 1915 and replaced by a hardliner from the CUP. Now, on being given orders to deport the Armenians in Erzerum, he stalled. Tahsin cabled Talaat on 15 May, claiming that the rationale of putting the Armenians somewhere where they could "do no harm" was flawed. He objected to the deportation order on the grounds the Armenians "work mainly in trade and industry, and many of them understand the consequences that a [resistance] movement initiated by themselves could have … Erzerum is a fortified city and a powerful garrison. Hence the Armenians cannot create problems. As for the districts, they are inhabited by Armenians in small numbers living in miserable conditions." Tahsin and Talaat had obviously previously discussed the idea of deportation prior to May 1915, as the governor appeared to be repeating earlier objections: "I had assured your Excellency that if we decided to deport the Armenians to the interior, we risked creating precisely the kind of danger for the army that we wished to spare it." Despite initially objecting, Tahsin caved, but as he pointed out to a colleague, "One can't deport sixty thousand people from the borders of the Caucasus to Baghdad or Mosul with mere words."

In nearly every Armenian population centre, the prelude to deportation was a demand from the authorities for the Armenians to hand in their weapons. When weapons were not forthcoming the response was often brutal. One child survivor from the Anatolian town of Yozgat remembers, "they searched all the houses for guns. If they didn't find one, then they would take the men of that family and imprison them … They placed my uncle on the floor and put nails through his toenails. So finally my father bought guns and took them in so they would release my uncle." It was a pattern repeated elsewhere. Alma Johansson, a Swedish nun in a German order in Mush in the far east of Turkey, saw the results of police arrests:

The worst tortures began … at the beginning of May. The people who were arrested were clamped into pieces of timber, their feet shod with nails like horses, their beards, eyelashes, their fingernails and teeth pulled out; they were hung upside down … Naturally, many of them died, but some of them received medical treatment and were sent to the missionaries and so we saw what happened. To stop the screaming from being heard during torture, drums and pipes were played around the jail.

The 500 Armenians arrested in Erzerum were taken to a jail in a town to the west and tortured there. Turkish gendarmes were already adept at assaulting suspects and

Armenians being marched to prison by Ottoman soldiers near Harput, April 1915. (Originally published by the American Red Cross)

famed for excessive use of the ancient torture of *bastinado*: beating the bare soles of the feet with sticks. In Roman times twenty strokes was the typically administered punishment, but many Armenians received more than a hundred until they fainted. Some of those who survived had to have their toes amputated. Ostensibly they were being coerced into revealing the locations of weapons caches, or revealing plots to revolt, but most of the gendarmes did not even bother to engage in the pretence of interrogation. In the *vilayet* of Harput, 800 men survived the brutality, after which they were led out into the desert. One unlikely survivor narrated what happened next to the U.S. consul in Harput, Leslie A. Davis. "The gendarmes began shooting them. After they had fired two or three rounds and killed most of the men the order was given to not waste any more cartridges, but to bayonet the rest." The man who survived was wounded and left for dead beneath a pile of bodies.

In Erzerum, the army took on the task of organizing the deportations, with none of the reluctance displayed by the region's governor. Tahsin was still far more gracious to the banished Armenians than almost any other governor; he gave them fifteen days' notice, allowed them to sell their property and to leave with household goods and some provisions. Armenians did occasionally manage to depart with belongings, but, as had happened to the residents of Zeitun, they were quickly robbed of all they had. A rich widow from Baibourt, a town west of Erzerum, who survived the genocide by converting to Islam, took as many valuables as she could with her.

> I took three horses with me, loaded with provisions. My daughter had some five-lira pieces around her neck, and I carried some twenty liras and four diamond rings on my person ... We had got only two hours away from home when bands of villagers and brigands in large numbers surrounded us and robbed us of all we had ... The brigands took all the good-looking women and carried them off on their horses. Very many women and girls were thus carried off into the mountains; among them my sister, whose one-year-old baby they threw away.

Some of the deportees had divined the fate that awaited them. A priest from a village near Erzerum smuggled a letter out, which eventually reached the German consul in the city.

Erzerum blanketed with snow.

Deportations of Armenians. The man in the foreground is a gendarme.

One evening at sundown in May, messengers came bearing the bad news and proclaimed the order for our banishment. Two hours later, all of us—old people and children, brides and girls, poor and crippled people—were outside under the open sky ... we saw our houses being plundered by the soldiers who were in the village, and by our neighbours ... We are starving, our animals are starving, our dead remain lying practically unburied along the way ... Who knows where we are going, perhaps to a black grave.

Reports from Erzerum were already reaching the German Embassy. On 20 May a German administrator messaged Wangenheim, "News [has] reached us that orders had been given to clear all the Armenians out of the entire Plain of Passin to the north of Erzerum and take them to the Terdjan area. I immediately inquired of the Vali [governor Tahsin] if this were right. The Vali confirmed the news and added that he himself did not agree much with this measure, but that it had been ordered by the army and he had to obey. He promised to be as lenient as possible in carrying it out." The administrator had visited some of the Armenians deported from the town and described their situation as "Sheer misery—great desperation and bitterness. The women threw themselves and their children in my horse's path and begged for help. The sight of these poor, moaning people filled me with pity ... The Armenian population considers the representative of the German Reich to be its only protection."

7. GERMANY AND THE ARMENIANS

Wangenheim did not see Germany's role as that of protector of the Armenians. He had also completely swallowed Talaat's claim that all the Turkish actions were merely undertaken to prevent an uprising. On 8 May he informed the German Chancellor, "Despite efforts by Armenian circles to diminish the significance of the riots which have broken over the past few weeks ... or to put the blame on measures taken by the Turkish authorities, there are increasingly more signs that this movement is more widespread than was thought up to now and is being encouraged from abroad with the help of Armenian revolutionary committees." He then mentioned Van and Zeitun by name, adding, "It cannot be denied that the Armenian movement has taken on a worrying character over the past few weeks, which has given the government cause to introduce severe repressive measures."

The German ambassador was made fully aware of the extent of the "repressive measures". He was also informed in real time of the spread of the deportations. As early as mid-April, a German missionary in Marash had written to the Embassy in desperation. "If you could see in what sort of a condition the people are arriving from Zeytun [sic]. One does not like to behold such misery ... Would it not be possible for the Embassy to do something about it? Because, as an ally of Turkey, we can hardly approve of this way of dealing with matters." A few weeks later, the German consul in Adana sent him an urgent message, stating, "The whole Armenian population in the Vilayet of Adana is extremely frightened due to the actions of the government. Hundreds of families are being exiled, the prisons are overfilled, and again early this morning several people were executed. With its barbaric methods, the government is obviously damaging the interest of the nation." Wangenheim's reply was short and brutal: "As regrettable and, in many respects, also detrimental to our interest as the persecution of the Armenian population is, however, the most recent events in the border provinces—such as the revolt in Van and other activities in the country's interior—do in fact justify the severe measures taken by the authorities."

In response to the pleas from the consul in Erzerum to put pressure on the Turks, Wangenheim allowed his diplomats only the minimum of leeway and stripped them of their only effective weapon: the fact that as wartime allies of the Turks they were the only foreign power to retain any diplomatic clout. "You are authorized to approach your local Supreme Command about the deportation of the Armenians ... to advocate humane treatment of the deported, defenceless people. However, you should keep your intervention within the limits of a piece of friendly advice." On 22 May, Wangenheim received another update from Erzerum, reporting that Turkish refugees who had fled the fighting in the east were occupying and plundering Armenian homes, "With the exception of the molesting rape of the Armenian women and girls, which is nothing unusual here, the behaviour of the gendarmes accompanying the expelled Armenians is otherwise little suited to ease the hard fate of the expellees. The gendarmes' behaviour could not be brusquer if it were directed at the subjects of enemy nations." The German ambassador was utterly unmoved. At the end of the month, he sent an official summarizing telegram to the German Foreign Office in Berlin, outlining his recommendations for the policy that should be taken by Germany.

> In order to curb Armenian espionage and to prevent new Armenian mass uprisings, Enver Pasha ... intends ... to resettle in Mesopotamia all those family from the recently insurgent Armenian [population] centres ... He urgently requests us not to hinder him in doing so. Of course, the Turkish measures will again cause great excitement in the whole of the enemy and will be used against us ... Also the measures will certainly mean great hardship for the Armenian population. But I am of the opinion that we should moderate the measures in their form, but not basically hinder them.

Wangenheim's support for the Turkish government flew directly in the face of the calls for action from the German diplomats on the ground, who openly declared the likely result. The German ambassador received the message from Trebizond that, "An evacuation of such a size is tantamount to a massacre because due to the lack of any kind of transportation, barely half of these people will reach their destination alive ... About 30,000 persons are affected by the deportations just in the Vilayet of Trebizond." The consul from Trabzon, a city on the Black Sea coast, asserted, "I share the opinion of all my colleagues that the transport of women and children borders on mass murder." Another cabled Wangenheim, "The countermeasures taken involve nothing less than the destruction or enforced Islamization of a whole people. The destination of those exiled from Samsun is said to be Urfa. It is certain that no Christian Armenian will reach this destination. According to news from the interior, there are already reports on the disappearance of the deported population of entire towns." The German ambassador also received another message from Scheubner-Richter, the

'Those of fell by the wayside'–an image of slaughtered Armenians on a roadside which Morgenthau included in *Ambassador Morgenthau's Story*.

administrator in Erzerum, this time calling for action on religious, as well as human-itarian grounds: "As the only representative of a Christian power, the Armenian pop-ulation sees its natural protector in me. Situation difficult and embarrassing." Again, Wangenheim tied the hands of his subordinates, replying, "I confirm my [previous] telegram ... and must regretfully refrain for the moment from interceding ... Also request that [you] ... take no further steps in this matter with the military authorities."

From the end of April throughout the whole of May, as deportations got underway across eastern Turkey, the German ambassador prevented German representatives from intervening. It is impossible to prove whether strong German opposition to the actions of the Turkish government before wholesale massacres had started would have made any difference, but Wangenheim's direct call for non-intervention on the part of Germany makes him complicit in the genocide that followed. In 1915, British, French and Russian diplomats had been expelled from Turkey, and America, as a neutral in the war, was only able to protect the interests of its own citizens. Germany, however, was not only an ally of the Ottoman Empire, but played a significant role

Armenian resistance at Urfa.

in training and supporting the Turkish army. If any nation was in a position to halt the first major genocide of the twentieth century it was Germany. The only possible, but still inexcusable explanation for Wangenheim's resistance is that he genuinely believed Talaat's claim that the Turks lived in fear of an Armenian uprising and that he saw the action against the Armenians an unfortunate incident of war. But his stance was bringing him into conflict with his colleagues. On 4 June, Rössler, the German consul in Aleppo, added his own pleas for action. In a borderline insubordinate cable to Wangenheim he wrote, "With all respect I again beg you to allow me to raise a protest. The larger part of the Armenian deportees are women. They would be defenceless and liable to be violated during transport ... Would it not be possible to deport only the men and leave the women and children in Aleppo?" Rössler's strength of feeling appears to have moved Wangenheim to at least some action: as a result, the German ambassador contacted Talaat. He told Rössler the next day, "The Minister of the Interior has agreed to make inquiries with the local Vali [governor] concerning the situation of the Armenians deported from there [Aleppo]."

Wangenheim did finally realize the full extent of the government's plan for the Armenians. But it was not because of the first-hand reports he was regularly receiving from his consuls; it was because Talaat let slip his true intentions. In a conversation with the Consul General at the Constantinople Embassy, Dr Johann Mordtmann, Talaat candidly admitted that the deportations were to be expanded to include other provinces and that the Turkish government intended to use the war to "make a clean sweep of internal enemies" without "being hindered" by diplomatic intervention. The German Embassy was suddenly spurred into action. A formal note of protest was sent to Talaat who "made a somewhat offended impression and promised a reply". Wangenheim then cabled the German Chancellor, taking a completely different tone:

> The expulsion of the Armenian population from their homes in the East Anatolian provinces and their relocation to other areas is being carried out ruthlessly ... Zeytun [sic] and surrounding areas ... have been completely cleared ... It has come to light that the banishment of the Armenians is not only motivated by military considerations. The Minister of the Interior, Talaat Bey, recently spoke about this without reservation to Dr. Mordtmann, who is currently employed by the Imperial Embassy. He [Talaat] said that the Porte [central government] is intent on taking advantage of the World War in order to make a clean sweep of internal enemies—the indigenous Christians—without being hindered in doing so by diplomatic intervention.

A few days later, Wangenheim finally allowed the consul in Erzerum to lodge a genuine complaint with the Turkish authorities and, this time, Wangenheim was instructing him to do so: "I would like to ask Your Excellency to point out to the Vali in a friendly but insistent manner that such ignominious occurrences damage the image of the government in neutral foreign countries and among Turkey's friends ... I will be making intercessions of a similar kind to the Porte." What Talaat and the other leaders of the Turkish government did not know was that the German protests would be brief and extremely limited and that the ambassador would not be around long to continue making them: Wangeheim was in fact gravely ill.

8. CRIMES AGAINST HUMANITY

As he did every Monday, on 7 June 1915 Morgenthau got into his diplomatic car at the front steps of the American Embassy and was driven down the hill towards the Golden Horn. The waterway would have been alive with boats on the early summer morning, the temperature a balmy twenty degrees: the perfect time of year. If he glanced across his shoulder as the car crossed the floating Galata Bridge, he would have seen half the city on the hill behind him: the multiple domes of the New Mosque looking down, flanked by low, grey-stone buildings. A few larger steamers would have flashed past the windows, the shouts of the crews dulled by the wash of the water flowing towards the sea and the cries of hungry gulls wheeling high above the masts and minarets. A century before, the seat of the Ottoman government had been the opulent Topkapi Palace, but now it was an Italian-style white-stone building just across the street; Morgenthau was paying his weekly visit to the Grand Vizier.

Technically, the Grand Vizier, or Chief Minister, outranked Talaat and Enver, but in fact Saim Halim was a primarily decorative fixture, much like the Sultan himself. Officially however, he remained the head of government and thus it was to the Grand Vizier that the Allies had addressed their letter. The problem was that because of the war, the British, Russian and French governments were without an embassy or an ambassador in Constantinople, so they had sent their letter from Paris, with the request that Morgenthau play the role of postman. The letter (dated 14 May 1915) was extremely forthright:

> For about a month the Kurd and Turkish populations of Armenia has been massacring Armenians with the connivance and often assistance of Ottoman authorities. Such massacres took place in middle April at Erzerum, Dertchun, Eguine, Akn, Bitlis, Mush, Sassun, Zeitun ... At the same time in Constantinople [the] Ottoman Government ill-treats [the] inoffensive Armenian population. In view of those new crimes of Turkey against humanity and civilization, the Allied governments announce publicly to the Sublime-Porte that they will hold personally responsible [for] these crimes all members of the Ottoman government and those of their agents who are implicated in such massacres.

Galata Bridge, across the Golden Horn, viewed from the US Embassy side in 1913.

The letter remains a remarkable piece of diplomacy. Completely devoid of tact—it was a diktat from a group of allies to their enemy in time of war—it nonetheless was a powerful statement that the actions against the Armenians, the full extent of which the British, French and Russian governments were not aware of, would not go unnoticed or unpunished. The Grand Vizier flew into a rage. Morgenthau recalled, his face flushed with anger and he began a long diatribe against the whole Armenian race. He declared that the Armenian 'rebels' had killed 120,000 Turks at Van. This and other of his statements were so absurd that I found myself spiritedly defending the persecuted race, and this aroused the Grand Vizier's wrath still further, and, switching from the Armenians, he began to abuse my own country, making the usual charge that our sympathy with the Armenians was largely responsible for all their troubles.

Morgenthau related the Grand Vizier's response to Washington, pointing out that all the while actions against the Armenians were intensifying, "[the] Grand Vizier ... expressed regret at being held personally responsible and resentment at attempted interference by foreign governments with the sovereign rights of the Turkish government over their Armenian subjects. Meanwhile persecution against Armenians increasing in severity ... twenty Armenians have been hanged here on ostensible charge of separatist conspiracy. Further executions said to be pending." Not long afterwards, the Turkish government sent its formal reply to the Allies. It was a vehement denial: "It is completely false that there have been massacres of Armenians in the Empire ... The accusations of the governments of the Triple Entente [Allies] on this subject are, thus, nothing but lies ... it is the agents of the Triple Entente, particularly those of Russia and England, who, taking advantage of every opportunity, excite the Armenian population to revolt."

Having begun the war technically as a neutral, Turkey was now fighting to push back British, French, Australian and New Zealand troops at Gallipoli on the Dardanelles peninsula, which had been invaded by the British in April 1915. The war was now closer to home and as a consequence Turkish ministers were even less inclined than they might have otherwise been to accept a reprimand from the 'Great Powers' who were now their enemies. Despite receiving a dressing down from the Grand Vizier, Morgenthau continued to remonstrate with those in authority.

On 19 June, the American ambassador and his Armenian interpreter, Schmavonian, paid a visit to Enver. The Minister of War was the exact physical opposite of the Minister of the Interior: where Talaat was brutish and broad-shouldered, Enver was wiry and refined. He seemed to Morgenthau "younger than his uniform ... an extremely neat and well-groomed object, with a pale, smooth face, made even more striking by his black hair, and with delicate white hands, and long, tapering fingers".

Ismail Enver, Minister for War.

The conversation was typically pleasant. "[Enver] said he is absolutely not opposed to the Armenians as a people, he has the greatest admiration for their industry, etc., but that, if they ally themselves with their enemies, as they did in the Van district, they would have to be destroyed ... He said it was all right during peace time to attempt platonic means to quiet Armenians and Greeks, but during war they have no time to investigate and negotiate ... He told me there would be no more massacres of Armenians." It was a bare-faced lie; only a few weeks before Enver had assured Morgenthau that he had halted the expulsion of Armenians from Erzerum. Enver presented himself as a realist: a man placed in an unfortunate position by the war, who would have coexisted peacefully with the Armenians if only it had been possible. It was a falsehood he managed to publicly maintain for nearly his entire time in office.

The following morning, Morgenthau and Enver went riding together through the forests surrounding the city. The pair again discussed the Armenians and Enver adamantly denied suggestions that Turkish soldiers had been mistreating women: "He could not believe that a Turkish soldier would maltreat a woman that had been confined," Morgenthau noted.

Many of those who witnessed first-hand the treatment of women and girls during the Armenian Genocide refrained from describing what they saw in detail. Among the testimonies of missionaries and even survivors, phrases such as 'you can imagine the fate of the women and girls' are commonplace. Even prior to the deportations, non-Turkish women were in a vulnerable situation and sexual violence against

Armenian women is frequently commented on in accounts of police searches for weapons. In the process of deportations, the rape of women appears in many cases to have been deliberate, rather than opportune. As early as March 1915 in a village in Tabriz, once soldiers had rounded up the men they "return[ed] to outrage the women and girls, not even little children being spared". An account from Urmia paints a similarly horrific picture, "A mother said that not a woman or girl above twelve (and some younger) ... escaped violation. This is the usual report from the villages ... Several women from eighty to eighty-five years old have suffered with the younger women." On the march, younger, prettier women were sometimes separated from groups and occasionally sold to Muslims in villages the convoys passed through, while soldiers and *chetes* supposedly guarding convoys violated women on an almost nightly basis. A deportee from Mush recounted, "All the old women and the weak who were unable to walk were killed. There were about one hundred Kurdish guards over us [originally a group of over 8,000], and our lives depended on their pleasure. It was a very common thing for them to rape our girls in our presence. Very often they violated eight, or ten-year-old girls, and as a consequence many were unable to walk and were shot."

As June drew to a close the full scale of the deportations was becoming apparent. When the entire Armenian community in Mesereh was ordered to go to Urfa, the American consul stationed in Harput, Leslie Davis, cabled Constantinople, "The full meaning of such an order can scarcely be imagined by those who are not familiar with the peculiar conditions of this isolated region. A massacre, however horrible the word may sound, would be humane in comparison with it. In a massacre many escape, but a wholesale deportation of this kind in this country means a lingering and perhaps even more dreadful death for nearly everyone." The German Embassy was receiving similar messages. The consul in Trebizond informed Wangenheim,

About 30,000 persons are affected by the deportation just in the Vilayet of Trebizond. A mass transport of this kind for hundreds of kilometres along routes that are lacking in accommodation and supplies, and where 300 kilometres must count as being completely infested with typhus fever, would claim enormous numbers of victims ... I am absolutely no friend of the Armenians, but I consider myself to be obliged to point out to Your Excellency the dangers of this mass deportation from the standpoint of humanity and prestige.

Turkish troops and a military band on a parade ground.

That the Turks were not deporting Armenians, but instead sending them on death marches was also becoming abundantly clear. A German Red Cross doctor in Erzindjan wrote to Rössler in June and the German consul in Aleppo forwarded the letter to Wangenheim:

> it was strange that no definite destination was given for the journey [of the deported Armenian families] ... traveling in Anatolia is not easy, even for wealthy people with horses, and it demands a healthy constitution. Furthermore, it is often difficult to find food for 20 people in the small villages along the way. How, then, are 20,000 or more women, children and old people to be fed for weeks in the heat of the sun, let alone finding accommodation for them. I never seriously believed the government's intention of doing so.

9. THE PROCESS OF THE DEPORTATIONS

The deportations were systematic and almost all followed the same pattern. The Armenian community in the village or town was ordered to leave at short notice; most seemed to believe the claim that they were being deported. One survivor recalled, "When they came to tell us to leave, they took us by surprise. Just three days before, we had gone to see the grapes to see if they were ripe enough to be blessed [by a priest]. Everything was so peaceful then. Only three days later, the town crier called out that we had to leave the town ... we had to get ready and sell whatever we could. Oh, all those beautiful things, antiques, rugs; we could not carry them with us." In Harput, Leslie Davis, the American consul, recorded, "we were all startled by the announcement that the Turkish Government had ordered the deportation of every Armenian, man, woman and child ... This announcement was made by the town crier ... who went around the streets, accompanied by a small boy beating a drum, and called out the terrible proclamation in a stentorian voice."

In some towns, the men—those too old for conscription or the small number who had succeeded in buying their way out of the draft—were rounded up first, but in all cases they were separated from the women and children. They would be the first to be killed.

One of a tiny number of survivors was Sarkis Manukian, an Armenian with a doctorate in philosophy from Leipzig university, who worked as a teacher in Erzerum. Women and children were marched on ahead and over 2,000 men held together in a valley. "The Kurds and the gendarmes explained to us, 'You will now die, but it is not our fault; the government demands it.' Each man was stripped and then ... Their heads were cut off with knives and axes and their corpses thrown into a chasm." Because Manukian spoke Kurdish he managed to persuade one of the Kurds to take pity on him and allow him to escape. His survival was nearly miraculous. The German consul in Adana, Eugen Buge, on a journey in the interior saw first-hand another typical massacre: "We were eyewitnesses as about one hundred Turkish soldiers shot several hundred Armenians from Yozgat and Sungurlu, all men ... they beat them to death with the butts of their rifles and annihilated all of them without exception."

The official line that the Armenians were going to be sent to the interior had an element of truth, for the women and children. The convoys were typically marched south from eastern Turkey, although those from the far east were moved west, before

Desperate deportees on the road.

heading south, and then towards modern-day Syria. They were destined to be gathered in camps at Aleppo and at Der-el-Zor in the middle of the desert. Many thousands died along the way from starvation, disease, or at the hands of their captors. One convoy of 18,000 that left Mamouret-ul-Aziz and Sivas was reduced to only 150 by the time it had travelled the 350 miles to Aleppo seventy days later. There was no compassion, even for pregnant women. A German civil servant working for the Baghdad Railway recalled: "They are hardly given enough time to give birth to their child. One woman had twins during the night. The next morning she had to move on on foot, carrying two children on her back. After marching for two hours she collapsed. She had to put the two children down under a bush and was forced by the soldiers to continue marching."

The numbers of those deported were almost impossible to assess. In early June, Jackson reported from Aleppo that "the total number of Armenians thus dispersed is almost 62,000; of whom 80% are women and children under 15 years of age". A likely far more accurate figure was provided by a German doctor, who attempted to complete an assessment of the total number of those exiled in the same month. He communicated to the German Foreign Office that "until now about 200,000 Armenians

An Armenian woman kneels beside her dead child in a field "within sight of help and safety at Aleppo".

have been affected by the deportation measures". These, he said, "paralleled only in the deportations of the ancient Assyrians, cannot be justified by military purposes; rather, they amount to the veiled massacre of Christians." An anonymous witness, whose accounts reached the American press in late summer, observed,

> Armenians of all the towns and all the villages of Cilicia have been deported *en masse* to the desert regions south of Aleppo ... The populations of Kaisaria, Diyarbakir, Ourfa [Urfa], Trebizond, Sivas, Harpout [Harput] and the district of Van have been deported to the deserts of Mesopotamia, from the southern outskirts of Aleppo as far as Mosul and Baghdad ... The exiles will have to traverse on foot a distance that involves one or two months' marching and sometimes even more, before they reach the particular corner of the desert assigned to them for their habitation, and destined to become their tomb. We hear, in fact, that the course of their route and the stream of the Euphrates are littered with the corpses of exiles, while those who survive are doomed to certain death, since they will find in the desert neither house, nor work, nor food. It is simply a scheme for exterminating the Armenian nation wholesale, without any fuss. It is just another form of massacre, and a more horrible form.

The American consul in Harput, Leslie Davis, decided to take matters into his own hands. Having already presented to the Embassy his view that "wholesale deportation of this kind in this country means a lingering and perhaps even more dreadful death for nearly everyone", he decided to personally save as many Armenians as he could. His actions risked his career and potentially his life. Harput had been home to Armenians since the Middle Ages, but from early June deportations began; the official line was that the Armenians were being moved 150 miles south across the desert to Urfa. Davis was adamant in a message to Morgenthau: "I do not believe it is possible for one in a hundred to survive, perhaps not one in a thousand." The city and surrounding towns were incredibly isolated. When Davis was first posted to Harput he travelled by wagon for thirteen days from the Black Sea port of Samsoun. To reach Constantinople required an eighteen-day ride on horseback and then a journey of three days by rail; even telegrams could take two weeks to arrive from the capital. At first Davis worked to secure a temporary stay on deportation for any Armenians who had any documents that had links to America, claiming they were potentially dual citizens. Many deposited valuables with him and when the deportations began in earnest, the consulate had acquired

over $200,000 in gold. Davis hid Armenian families in the walled garden of the consulate, around twenty people at time, under the shade of forty mulberry trees. When a young Turkish boy the consul employed to buy food began to make inquiries about the sudden surge in bread consumption, Davis took it upon himself to go to the market each day to purchase food for his charges. He continued to lobby the governor, who surprisingly said he would halt the deportations, but only if Davis would sign a document confirming that all the Armenians deported were "guilty of some offence". He refused. In all, he sheltered eighty Armenians over

Leslie A. Davis, U.S. Consul in Harput.

a period of two years at the height of the genocide, placing them in safe houses elsewhere in Turkey and smuggling others along the Euphrates river to Russia.

Davis himself rode out on horseback several times along the deportation route. His worst fears were realized. "After about two hours we arrived at a large valley. Here there were more dead bodies than I had seen in any other place on either trip. We estimated that there were not less than two thousand in one valley." In all, he assessed he had seen 10,000 bodies in valleys near one lake alone. He later remembered, "A remarkable thing about the bodies that we saw was that nearly all of them were naked ... There were gaping bayonet wounds on most of the bodies, usually in the abdomen or chest, sometimes in the throat. Few persons had been shot, as bullets were too precious ... nearly all of the women lay flat on their backs and showed signs of barbarous mutilation by the bayonets of the gendarmes." In Davis's view, the Armenian Genocide was "probably the most terrible tragedy that has ever befallen any people in the history of the world".

The German consul in Aleppo was sending similarly forthright messages. Having seemingly given up on the German Embassy, Rössler summarized what was happening in a direct message to the Chancellor himself:

> The Turkish government has driven its Armenian subjects, the innocent ones, mark you, into the desert in thousands upon thousands ... exempting neither the sick nor pregnant women nor the families of conscripted men, has given them food and water in insufficient quantities and irregularly, has done nothing against the epidemics which have broken out amongst them, has driven women to such desperation that they set their babies and newborns by the wayside, has sold their adolescent daughters ... left them to the mercy of their guards and therefore to dishonour ... arranged for the murders of the representatives of whom it sent into exile. It has released prisoners from the prisons, put them in soldiers' uniforms and sent them to areas where the deportees would be passing through. It has called up Circassian volunteers and set them on the Armenians. But what does it offer as semi-official explanations? 'The Ottoman government ... is extending its benevolent protection to all honest Christians living peacefully in Turkey ...' I was not able to believe my own eyes when I saw this explanation and I can find no words to describe the depths of its untruth.

There were considerably fewer Armenians in western Turkey, but populations were still deported to Aleppo and the other staging posts, in many cases by train.

THE BASES OF CIVILIZA
'ION IN THE NEAR EAST ARM
ENIAN CRANES & OURFA
1914 - 1919

Skulls of Armenians massacred at Urfa, surrounded by Armenian dignitaries and women from the women's shelter in Urfa's Monastery of St Sarkis, June 1919.

In total, around 330,000 people from Thrace, the Dardanelles and Constantinople itself, as well as adjoining westerly regions, were sent towards the desert. Jackson, in Aleppo, kept a ledger of those who arrived by train, counting 23,675 women and 9,076 children as of 31 August 1915. Anna Birge, an American whose husband was a teacher in Smyrna, witnessed the westerly deportations when she travelled by train from Smyrna to Constantinople in 1915. "At every station where we stopped, we came side by side with one of these trains. It was made up of cattle-trucks, and the faces of little children were looking out from behind the tiny barred windows of each truck … one could plainly see old men and old women, young mothers with tiny babies … all huddled together like so many sheep or pigs—human beings treated worse than cattle are treated." Anna and her husband met a German officer on the train, who described what he had seen in the interior. "Hundreds of people were walking over the mountains, driven by soldiers. Many dead and dying by the roadside … Babies lying dead in the road. Human life thrown away everywhere." Seeing the trains had a profound impact on Anna, who wrote down what she had witnessed when she returned home to Massachusetts and sent her account to an organization helping refugees. "The last thing we saw late at night and the first thing in the morning was one train after another carrying its freight of human lives to destruction … The crying of those babies and little children for food is still ringing in my ears."

10. "THEY CAN LIVE IN THE DESERT"

On 8 July 1915, Morgenthau visited Wangenheim who told his American opposite number that he was about to go on holiday. In reality, he was returning to Germany for medical treatment. They spoke "about the Armenian matter" and Wangenheim told Morgenthau that he "had sent a protest". Wangenheim's official complaint was in Morgenthau's eyes solely done to put German objections on record. The American ambassador forever held the view that Wangenheim had done nothing but the absolute bare minimum for the Armenians, writing three years later, "He [Wangenheim] did not talk to Talaat or Enver, the only men who had any authority, but to the Grand Vizier, who was merely a shadow." Morgenthau's assessment of Wangenheim's efforts was accurate. The German ambassador continued to pass directly to the Chancellor updates on the massacres and first-hand reports, but his own added notes to these communications betray their purpose. One note, attached to a communique in mid-July 1915 read, "If I have recently reported in greater detail about these occurrences to Your Excellency, then this was done under the presumption ... our enemies will later accuse us of being accomplices. With the help of my reports, we will be in a position to prove to the hostile world at an appropriate time, in particular through the press, that we have always expressly condemned the exaggerated measures of the Turkish government and even more so the excesses of local official bodies."

On 10 July Morgenthau again telegrammed the Secretary of State:

Persecution of Armenians assuming unprecedented proportions. Reports from widely scattered districts indicate systematic attempt to uproot peaceful Armenian populations through arbitrary arrests, terrible tortures, wholesale expulsions and deportations from one end of the Empire to the other accompanied by frequent instances of rape, pillage, and murder, turning into massacre, to bring destruction and destitution on them ... directed from Constantinople in the name of military necessity ... Many Armenians are becoming Muslims to avoid persecution ... The only Embassy here which might assist in lessening these atrocities is the German but I believe it will simply content itself with giving advice and a formal protest probably intended for the record and to cover itself from future responsibility ...

> I have conferred with the various American missionaries now here ... all agree that the crisis is worse than 1895 and 1896 massacres but none of them could suggest any further steps than those I have already taken. I fear the matter will have to run its course.

Morgenthau was desperate for the United States to take action, although even the ambassador was at a loss as to what could be done. His protestations were even drawing criticism from other foreigners; a German Jew appealed to him "as one Jew to another" to think of the impact to his career. Morgenthau is said to have replied, "[then] go ahead and have me recalled. If I am to suffer martyrdom, I can think of no better cause in which to be sacrificed. In fact, I would welcome it, for I can think of no greater honour than to be recalled because I, a Jew, have been exerting all my powers to save the lives of hundreds of thousands of Christians." Anxious to receive a reply to his 10 July message, Morgenthau sent a follow-up to the Secretary of State six days later. "It appears that a campaign of race extermination [against the Armenians] is in progress under a pretext of reprisal against rebellion ... I believe nothing short of actual force which obviously the United States are not in a position to exert would adequately meet the situation." The Secretary of State's reply to Morgenthau's earlier telegram crossed his chaser in the wires. It read, "[State] Department approves your procedure in pleading with Turkish Minister of Interior and Minister of War to stop Armenian persecution and in attempting to enlist sympathies of German and Austrian ambassadors in this cause. The Department can offer no additional suggestions."

As Leslie Davis had witnessed, massacres were taking place on a vast scale, accompanying the deportations. In Diyarbakir Mehmed Resid appeared to have decided to exterminate the entire Armenian population without the pretence of transporting them anywhere at all. The German consul in Aleppo received an eyewitness report stating, "In Besniye, the entire population of about 1,800 women and children and only a few men was deported; they were supposed to be transported to Urfa. By the River Goeksu, a tributary of the Euphrates, they had to take off their clothes, were then all massacred and thrown into the river." The entire town of Djezire was massacred by Kurds who, the consul was told, "had been hired for this purpose by Resid Bey". On 31 July, Wangenheim cabled the Chancellor, "Since the beginning of this month, the vali of Diyarbakır, Resid Bey, has begun the systematic extermination of the Christian population in his province, without distinguishing between race or creed."

An eyewitness recounted that many of the bodies left by the roadside had been mutilated. Pictured is the corpse of a young Armenian man.

The massacres were worst in the far eastern regions. At Mush, the Swedish nun who had helped treat men tortured by the gendarmes in May also witnessed the massacres a few months later. "The women were taken with the children to the next villages, locked by the hundred into houses and burned [alive]. Others were thrown into the river ... There had been about 25,000 Armenians in Mush; in addition, Mush has 300 villages, most of which had been Armenian. When we left Mush after three weeks, everything was burned down."

Corpses were floating down the Tigris and Euphrates rivers. The German consul in Mosul noted on 10 June, "For several days now, corpses and human members have been floating down the river," while in Aleppo, Rössler recounted that bodies were seen in the river for twenty-five straight days, "all tied together in the same way, in pairs, back to back". After a short break they then began seeing the bodies of women and children. The bodies that washed up on the bank were eaten by vultures and wild dogs. When Turkish authorities sent a complaint to Resid Bey, upstream in Diyarbakir he placed the blame elsewhere: "The Euphrates has very little to do with our vilayet.

The bones of Armenians burned alive by Turkish soldiers in Sheykhalan, in the province of Mush. Discovered by Russian soldiers (pictured) in 1915.

The corpses coming down the river have probably come from the provinces of Erzerum and Harput. Those who drop dead here are either thrown into deep abandoned caves or, as often happens, cremated. There is rarely any reason to bury them."

Protestations from foreign nationals—Germans and Americans being the only ones permitted to remain following the outbreak of war—continued to reach diplomats in impressive numbers, given the restrictions put in place on most communications. From April 1915, Morgenthau had been stopped from communicating in code with his consuls and mail had been censored, hence why so many accounts were delivered in person to the German and American representatives in the provinces. A group of German residents in the town of Konia, one of the rail terminals for deportees, sent a joint a letter to the German Embassy. It was signed by a school teacher, an engineer working on the Baghdad Railway, and the Chairman of an industrial trading company.

The undersigned German nationals, at present residing in Konya [sic], would herewith like to present the following report to the Imperial German Embassy ... we have been witnesses of the most moving scenes, which anyone not coming into close contact with them can hardly imagine. Every day long trains of Armenians arrive here, who according to their accounts, have been deported from Ismid, Adapazar and the surrounding areas. From some of those passing through we have learned that the deportation regulations have already been enforced for many months in Cilicia and North Mesopotamia and as we hear, also other places in Anatolia are being cleared of the Armenians ... The whole of the route from here to beyond Aleppo resembles a caravan of misery and wretchedness. In places such as Karaman, Eregli and Bozanti, where the people themselves are suffering from a shortage of bread, the fate of the deportees is unimaginable; they are destined to suffer a slow, agonizing death by starvation ... The whole measure seems to be aimed at a complete extermination of the Armenians. We Germans, who are forced daily to observe this inhumane activity, feel it is our duty as members of a cultural state in the midst of a half-civilized people, to protest against it.

German workers building a station at Aleppo for the Baghdad Railway.

In early August, Talaat invited Morgenthau for a private meeting. Talaat began in good humour, remarking that Morgenthau had shaved his beard. He joked, "You have become a young man again. You are so young now that I cannot go to you for advice any more." Morgenthau was not amused: "I have shaved my beard," he replied, "because it has become very gray—made gray by your treatment of the Armenians."

A deflated Talaat informed Morgenthau that he had invited him over to discuss that very thing. He began, "I can explain our position on the whole Armenian subject." Talaat stated three 'objections' to the Armenians. "In the first place, they have enriched themselves at the expense of the Turks. In the second place, they are determined to domineer over us and to establish a separate state. In the third place, they have openly encouraged our enemies ... We have therefore come to the irrevocable decision that we shall make them powerless before this war is ended." Morgenthau vehemently disagreed on every aspect, but Talaat was insistent: "It is no use to argue, we have already disposed of three quarters of the Armenians; there are now none left in Bitlis, Van and Ezeroum." After this startling admission, he added, "The hatred between the Turks and the Armenians is now so intense we have got to finish with them." Morgenthau changed tack. "If you are not influenced by humane considerations, think of the material loss. These people are your businessmen ... very large tax payers." The Minister of the Interior was unmoved. "We care nothing about the commercial loss. We have figured all that out and we know it will not exceed five million pounds." Not only had the leading figures of the Ottoman government planned to exterminate the Armenians, they had even costed it to around two and a half Turkish pounds per head. Morgenthau pleaded with Talaat, who shut him down. "I have asked you to come here so as to let you know our Armenian policy is absolutely fixed and that nothing can change it. We will not have the Armenians anywhere in Anatolia. They can live in the desert but nowhere else."

Above: An Armenian woman in traditional dress, poses on a hillside in Artvin, c. 1910.

Right: Armenian women from Gandzak (Azerbaijan), pre-1917.

Turkish troops in action at the battle of Qatia, Sinai, where they defeated the British in 1915.

Military supplies piled up at Anzac Cove, Gallipoli, May 1915.

V Beach at Helles, Gallipoli.

The Young Turks enter Constantinople, 1909.

After the comprehensive defeat by the Russians at Sarikamish, desperate Turkish stragglers make for Erzerum, October 1914.

Armenians with spinning wheels and cotton, Erivan, c. 1915.

Above: Armenian refugee children paddling in the sea near Marathon, Greece, c. 1915.

Left: Armenian refugees in Marsovan, Turkey, near the Black Sea.

Armenian orphans at a Near East Relief facility in Syria.

A Near East Relief camp in the Turkish countryside, December 1919.

Above left: Armenian children in Baghdad, 1918.

Above right: An Armenian and Syrian Relief Campaign fundraising poster.

Below: An Armenian orphanage in Aleppo, 1920.

Right: Armenian street children, mid-1920s.

Below: The text on the left-hand-side reads: "Taken: 3/8/1919: ARMENIAN REFUGEES WHO ARRIVED IN UNITED STATES. Armenian refugees who were among the most prosperous families of Harpoot and who fled Turkey to escape the atrocities of Turks. The party which arrived at San Francisco, is led by Sooren Darkaspirin, a nineteen year old lad, [the] only [one] of [the] party who speaks the English language, is second from the right."

An Armenian and Syrian Relief Campaign fundraising poster.

Above left: Four Armenian women photographed at a rescue home in the early 1920s, having just escaped slavery. Their relief is palpable.

Above right: Lady Anne Azgapetian, wife of General Azgapetian, of Armenia, with her daughter Araxia, at the convention of the National Woman's Party in Washington DC, February 1921.

Right: The Armenian Genocide memorial church in Der-el-Zor, which was destroyed by Islamic State in 2014.

11. THE CONCENTRATION CAMPS

It would have been far more accurate of Talaat to have stated that, rather than being permitted to live in the desert, the Armenians were being left there to die. Outside of Aleppo and along the river Euphrates, tens of thousands of Armenian deportees were gathered in concentration camps, although the 'camps' were simply open-air spaces where deportees had congregated or been herded, sometimes with flimsy tents for cover, often with nothing. By August 1915 there were 23,000 in the Euphrates camps; six months later there would be 310,000.

There were also large numbers of deportees in the area around Aleppo. At the start of the deportations, thousands congregated in the city itself. The overcrowding, squalor and almost total lack of any assistance from the Turkish government—a few convoys from Cilicia were given food, but most were just left to fend for

Tent camp in the Syrian desert, one of a collection of images secretly taken and smuggled out by Armin T. Wegner, a German second lieutenant stationed in Ottoman Turkey in 1915–16.

themselves—meant that the refugee areas quickly became incubators for disease. Typhoid fever and typhus were rife. A German teacher travelled to some of the areas in the city where Armenians had congregated. "I visited every part of the city in which Armenians—what was left of the columns of deportees—were to be found ... I found piles of putrefying dead bodies ... sick and starving people left to fend for themselves ... Opposite our school ... were the remnants of the one of these columns of deportees, around four hundred emaciated creatures, among whom were some one hundred children between the ages of five and seven. Most were suffering from typhus or dysentery." Another foreign observer recounted:

> One sees them [the deportees] in Aleppo on pieces of waste ground, in old buildings, courtyards and alleyways, and their condition is simply indescriba-ble. They are totally without food and are dying of starvation. If one looks into these places where they are living one simply sees a huddled mass of dying and dead, all mixed up with discarded, ragged clothing, refuse and human excrement, and it is impossible to pick out any one portion and describe it as being a living person. A number of open carts used to parade the streets, looking out for corpses, and it was a common sight to see one of these carts pass contain-ing anything up to ten or twelve human bodies, all terribly emaciated.

There were also camps outside the city, where the evacuees were in an even worse state. When cholera broke out in September, the Turkish authorities began evacuating the city and shipping around 5,000 Armenians each week further east. Others were simply driven out of the city towards the desert. The Sibel camp, situated on a wide plain leading towards the Syrian desert, was always crammed with several thousand refugees, but each day, one convoy arrived at the camp, while another left it, heading east. Each morning the bodies of those who had died in the night were collected and flung into a ditch. Another camp had 500 tents, but housed 3,000 deportees; Jackson estimated there were a hundred deaths there every day.

Jackson personally witnessed more of the genocide than any of his American diplo-matic colleagues. Although Leslie Davis found and photographed thousands of bod-ies in the desert, the American consul in Aleppo had to watch column after column of evacuated Armenians arrive, either to die of disease or be force-marched onwards from Aleppo. Jackson facilitated assistance for the Armenians, even partnering with the German consul, Rössler, to pressure the governor to allow the opening of both an orphanage for Armenian children and a hospital to treat deportees; the hospital was

Women living in the streets.

by this time a necessity as a result of the typhus outbreak. The orphanage was located in a large house right next to the German Consulate and had been donated by a Swiss businessman. Despite the efforts and intentions of the Turkish authorities, Armenian refugees were receiving help and their plight was also being publicized.

On Friday 24 September 1915, *The New York Times* splashed the headline "500,000 Armenians Said To Have Perished. Washington Asked to Stop Slaughter of Christians by Turks and Kurds" across its front page. The week before, a group of missionaries and millionaires had gathered together to do something to help. The men convened at the insistence of James L. Barton, a sixty-year-old former Turkish missionary who now chaired the American Board of Commissioners for Foreign Missions. On 14 September, the erudite Quaker had written to his friend, the wealthy businessman and confidant of the President, Cleveland H. Dodge, suggesting a gathering at Dodge's office because, "The Armenians have no one to speak for them and it is without question a time when the voice of Christianity should be raised". On the morning of 16 September, Barton, Dodge and a few friends met and discussed the events unfolding in Turkey. That morning they decided to create a new

Morgenthau (left) meeting members of the New York Committee for Armenian and Syrian Relief on his return in February 1916. Pictured are Samuel Dutton (centre) and Cleveland Dodge (right).

organization to intervene to help the Armenians. They called it the Armenian Relief Committee. Immediately they began raising money and collecting information from contacts in Turkey; in less than a month the Armenian Relief Committee had brought in $70,000 (equivalent to £600,000 in today's money).

The publicity and the apparent ease with which Americans in particular were getting information to the outside world annoyed Talaat. He cabled his brother-in-law in late 1915, "The American Consuls are obtaining information by secret means ... [it is] crucial to our policy of the moment to convince foreigners travelling in that area [Aleppo] that the sole purpose of this deportation is to change people's places of residence." He then added, in a macabre turn of phrase, "apply the known methods only in localities where they are appropriate". Others were less cryptic. Ahmed Eyub Sabri was a Turkish administrator sent from Constantinople to Aleppo in June 1915 to coordinate the deportations. In a discussion with a German diplomat, Sabri was seemingly perplexed by the man's failure to grasp their intentions. Sabri told him, "You still don't understand what we want; we want to eradicate the Armenian name."

The members of the Armenian Relief Committee—which was swiftly renamed the American Committee for Armenian and Syrian Relief—were not the only ones working hard to ensure that the real plans of Talaat and the Turkish government were made known. A former British ambassador to the United States, Viscount James Bryce, was also making an undiplomatic scene. Bryce urged his contacts in the United States to take action and at the same time began lobbying the British government. On 28 July 1915, he raised a written question in the House of Lords, inquiring "whether His Majesty's Government have any information regarding the massacres of the Christian inhabitants which are reported to have been committed by the Turks in the districts of Zeitun, Mush, Diarbekir [sic], Bitlis, and elsewhere in the region inhabited by the Armenians". The Foreign Office representative admitted in reply, "the information in the possession of the Foreign Office on the subject which my noble friend has raised, although it is not much more ample than that of which he is possessed, is in conformity with what he has told us. I fear that there can be no doubt that the general facts are as my noble friend has described them." Bryce continued to ask questions in Parliament, garnered coverage in the press and as support grew, the government commissioned him to compile a record of what was taking place. Together with a young British historian just out of university, Bryce would put together an extensive, verified and authoritative collection of eyewitness accounts of the genocide and would publish it while the genocide was still underway. But even though an international movement to assist the Armenians was gathering pace, the situation on the ground for the deportees remained desperate.

With the exception of the hospital Jackson and Rössler had lobbied to create, evacuees in Aleppo were just left to die. The authorities were forced to create new cemeteries, but the bodies piled up before graves could be dug. Rössler wrote that in one case, "before the authorities could begin to bury the dead there, the corpses were dumped in it in one big pile and lay out in the open for several days." Refugees were still being driven towards Aleppo, occasionally halting near other towns, such as Aintab, around sixty-five miles north of Aleppo city. Having spent months treating Turkish soldiers at a hospital in Constantinople, whom he described as "patient and grateful fellows, for the most part", in October, Dr Shepard finally managed to return to his hospital in Aintab.

While in Constantinople he had met Morgenthau on multiple occasions. On his final morning, Morgenthau, Gates (president of Robert College) and the doctor had

Displaced Armenian refugees in a camp at Aintab, following the 1909 massacre.

met to discuss how best to distribute relief aid; Morgenthau told Shepard to spend as much as he needed to at Aintab. Once he had returned, Shepard worked an extremely busy schedule of surgery, but still dedicated as much time as he could to aiding the Armenians around Aintab, who had not yet been moved on. Every other day, he went to a complex of half-built houses where hundreds were taking shelter and treated Armenian refugees infected with typhus. The disease is spread by lice, as they feed on the blood of their hosts, and the onset of the fever is usually quick, although death is accompanied by fits of coughing, severe muscle pain and spreading black spots. When Shepard realized that, despite taking precautions, he was infected, his response was typically sanguine: "If the Lord spares me, I shall be immune to fight the epidemic which is sure to follow in the winter." He was not spared and less than a fortnight later, his body was buried on the grounds of his hospital in a cheap coffin. Shepard's wife recounted that one Armenian said, "I have never seen Jesus, but I have seen Doctor Shepard."

12. THE ASSYRIAN AND PONTIC GENOCIDES

Armenians were not the only ones targeted for extermination by the Turkish government. The genocide extended to Assyrian and other Christian groups as well.

The initial threat of the Turkish offensive on the eastern border at Sarikamlish in early 1915 led the Russians to pull back their forces from northwestern Persia. In January, they retreated from the predominantly Assyrian region of Urmia. Turkish soldiers and Kurdish *chetes* immediately occupied the vacated area and set about sacking Christian villages. The treatment was remarkably similar to that being meted out to Armenians and other Christians near Van around the same time, months before the genocide formally began with the roundup of Armenian notables in Constantinople. But this time there was never even the threat of a potential revolt as a pretext. A Lazarist monk in Urmia, who kept a diary of the events, wrote that the whole region was in mourning: "For the hundreds of innocents tied together in groups of five or six, shot in the most cowardly way, stabbed, stoned to death, buried alive, thrown into wells ... the mourning of unfortunate mothers who have had their little girls of eight to ten violated by brutes ... our virgins sold at the bazar for ... not even the price of a piece of livestock ... Out of 40,000 people, 10,000 are missing, and the others are reduced to a state of beggary, their houses burned, their possessions taken away." Along with Armenians, Assyrians in eastern Anatolia and in Urmia sought refuge behind the Russian lines throughout the war, but as Russian fortunes waxed and waned, the frontiers of safety shifted. Thousands who fled in fear perished on the road.

The Assyrian Christian community concentrated in the historical region of Hakkari numbered around 100,000 at the outbreak of the war. When attacks began, they evacuated en masse into the mountains and fought back. Men and women, armed with archaic flintlock muskets in the face of modern rifles, resisted for more than two and a half months. From October 1915, groups crossed the high mountains into Persia, but only around half the Assyrian community from Hakkari reached safety behind the Russian lines. A Russian Embassy staff member, who worked as an interpreter in Constantinople until he was expelled at the start of the war, later wrote, "Without the slightest pretext of provocation, the Turkish government put the land of the Syriac [Assyrian] Christians of Hakkari to fire and the sword." It was part of "the odious plan of the Turkish leadership to rid itself of all Christians in the Empire". Elsewhere, in and around Van itself and in towns such as Diyarbakir and Harput, Assyrians were deported and massacred along with the Armenians.

Like the Turkish government's census, the only distinction of note was religion and to be 'Turkish' was to be Muslim. In an account seen by the German consul in Adana, a German national reported, "The inner circle around the Grand Vizier is extremely chauvinistic; every non-Muslim is described as a 'sales gens' [filthy person]; it was admitted to me that the Armenians needed to be exterminated to the last child, but it appears as if they wish the same for all other Christians. 'Turkey for the Turks' is the slogan."

A widowed Armenian woman who fled the massacres of 1894–96 after her husband was killed.

This demeaning view of non-Muslims was not an invention of Talaat and his cronies. Neither was it merely the outworking of an irrational hatred of the 'other'. It was the ultimate conclusion of the second-class status ascribed to non-Muslims under Islamic *Sharia* law. Conquered non-Muslim citizens within an Islamic state could be granted *dhimmi* status. Typically, the designation was applied to Christians and Jews who, in exchange for payment of a specific tax, were permitted to live and practise their religion behind closed doors. At the start of the eighteenth century, the *dhimmi* tax provided forty-five percent of the Ottoman government's revenue. Far from being a 'protected status', which is how *dhimmitude* is often described, *dhimmis* in the Ottoman Empire were at best second-class citizens. Their lower status was not just theoretical. They were banned from many higher-level jobs and these restrictions were one of the reasons that before the genocide so many educated Armenians living in cities had turned their hand to trade. In 1580, the then Sultan of the Ottoman Empire decreed that Jews and Christians should wear particular clothing. Although enforcement waned, Mustafa III reasserted the practice in 1758: Jews were made to wear red hats and Christians black, but never the traditional Turkish fez, which was reserved for Muslims. In appearance it was decreed they were to "preserve an attitude of humility in their demeaner", a position reinforced by regulations that required them to travel on donkeys, not horses. The same year, the Sultan, walking around Constantinople, saw a Jew and an Armenian Christian wearing forbidden clothing and promptly ordered them both to be beheaded. An English traveller in Palestine, which remained part of the Ottoman Empire until late in the First World War, recounted in 1816, "we met a party of Jews on asses ... conceiving me, from my Turkish dress ... to be a Mohammadan, they all dismounted and passed by us on foot. These persecuted people are held in such opprobrium here, that it is forbidden for them to pass a musselmen [Muslim] mounted, while Christians are suffered to do so either on mules or asses."

Dhimmitude was a centuries-old practice enshrined in Islam. The abolition of the *dhimmi* tax in the Ottoman Empire—largely as a result of pressure from Western governments—in the late nineteenth century did not abolish hundreds of years of entrenched religious prejudice. For Turkish politicians brought up on stories from their forebears of *dhimmis* dismounting when Muslims rode by, it was hardly surprising that they viewed such non-Turks as 'filthy'.

Christians slated for deportation from 1915 onwards were typically permitted to escape death if they converted to Islam and an unknown number, potentially many thousands, did so. Most men were still murdered, but women could survive by

Armenian orphans boarding a ship in Constantinople in 1915—among a lucky few who were permitted to be evacuated on humanitarian grounds.

accepting an offer to convert, usually accompanied by the requirement of marrying a Muslim or joining a harem, a custom that still existed in the Ottoman Empire in the early twentieth century. This practice of what effectively amounted to forced conversion—given the alternative was usually death—was extended to many thousands of Christian orphans who were brought up as Muslims, never to know their heritage. Some Armenians appear to have viewed conversion as a simple piece of paperwork—thousands of pre-filled conversion papers were distributed by CUP authorities—but for others it was a heart-rending choice. An Armenian survivor who converted and later found refuge in Syria recalled that one group of women from Samsoun were only persuaded to convert by fellow Armenians with "great difficulty: 'If we were going to become Turks we could have saved our husbands and children,' they would say. 'They gave their lives so that we wouldn't change our religion. How can we now become Muslims to save our lives when they were killed under the most dreadful circumstances.'"

The religious motivation is highlighted again and again by those who witnessed the genocide. The American consul in Harput, Leslie Davis, who sheltered Armenian families in the garden of the Consulate, recalled, "While these people were hiding in the Consulate the Turks were holding prayer meetings every night in the square in front of it and we could all hear them piously calling upon Allah to bless them in their efforts to kill the hated Christians." He also observed the targeted destruction of Christian property when he travelled along the route of the deportations.

> All of the purely Armenian villages were in ruins and deserted ... In the others, Armenian homes were empty. Everywhere it was a scene of desolation and destruction. The houses were crumbling to pieces and even the Christian churches ... had been pulled down. In the neighbouring village of Yegheki a large [church] bell which had only recently been purchased in America through the Consulate at Harput and put in place was lying in the debris of the church. The Mohammedans in their fanaticism seemed determined not only to exterminate the Christian population but to remove all traces of their religion.

A collection of eyewitness accounts of the murder of Assyrians, published in English after the war, contained a foreword by Viscount Bryce. In it, the British politician and humanitarian wrote, "It was the suffering of the Armenians that chiefly drew the attention of Britain and America because they were the most numerous ... and the slaughter was, therefore, on a large scale. But the minor communities, such as the

A caravan of 5,000 Greek Orthodox refugees.

Armenian refugees rescued by a French cruiser, 1915.

Nestorians and Assyro-Chaldean churches, were equally the victims of the plan for exterminating Christianity, root and branch, although the Turks had never ventured to allege that these communities had given any ground of offence." In all it is thought that up to 300,000 Assyrian and Chaldean Christians may have perished along with the Armenians in the genocide. The planned murder also extended to Greek Christian communities, who were primarily located in western Turkey. However, a detailed account of what is known as the Pontic Genocide is sadly outside the scope of this narrative.

The violence meted out toward the Assyrians and other Christians from 1915 onwards demonstrates the clear intent of the Turkish authorities to eradicate not just one ethnic group (the Armenians), but the followers of an entire religion who lived on Turkish soil. The Armenian Genocide, in that it included the slaughter of hundreds of thousands of other Christians, was predominantly therefore religious, rather than ethnic, cleansing. As Morgenthau wrote in his 1918 account: "The Armenians are not the only subjects in Turkey who have suffered from this policy of making Turkey exclusively the country of the Turks. The story which I have told about the Armenians, I could also tell ... about the Greeks and the [As]Syrians."

13. DEPARTURES

The immediate fundraising success of the American Committee for Armenian and Syrian Relief was swiftly communicated to Morgenthau. He was contacted by the Committee who offered to send between $50,000 and $100,000 to provide assistance for Armenian refugees. Schmavonian and Morgenthau took a morning walk in the garden of the deserted British Embassy to discuss how best to respond. At midday, Morgenthau replied: "Can use most advantageously one hundred thousand dollars and more ... When money assured I shall also use consuls of Aleppo and Damascus as distributors." He concluded, "One hundred thousand dollars carefully administered will make a good start but will not suffice. I implore my friends to do their utmost to assist liberally."

The American ambassador continued to hound the Turkish government about the Armenians. Morgenthau pressured Enver, going to see the Minister for War in person and alone. Enver admitted the Turkish government had deported as many as half a million Armenians from their homes, but was "not certain if they [the Turkish authorities] can furnish bread to the Armenians through winter". The American ambassador tried again to recruit support from the German Embassy. In the first week of October 1915, he telephoned Wangenheim to arrange a meeting to discuss the Armenians. The German ambassador visited Morgenthau at the American Embassy. Morgenthau wrote in his diary, "The man is absolutely broken in health. He has neuralgia on his right eye and twitches continually." Morgenthau's German counterpart expressed, yet again, the view "[the] Armenians had shown themselves as enemies of the Turks, that the two peoples could never live together". He then proposed a revealing solution to what he referred to as the "Armenian question". He told Morgenthau the Americans "ought to take some of them [the Armenians] to America, and Germany would send some to Poland and send Jewish Poles here [to Turkey] if they agreed not to work Zionist schemes". Wangenheim's view of the Jews was remarkably similar to Talaat's view of the Armenians: the German ambassador claimed they were "not desirable citizens".

German diplomats were now being slammed in the British press. At the start of October 1915, the London newspaper the *Westminster Gazette* told its readers, "Massacres of Armenians continue all over Turkey. It is estimated that there are up to now more than 800,000 victims ... not only have Government done nothing to prevent these massacres, but it appears to be established that in many towns the German

Consuls have taken a part in organizing them." The German Foreign Office was livid. The Under Secretary of State, Arthur Zimmerman, angrily messaged Wangenheim to attempt to stop anything similar appearing in American newspapers. "Please tell your American colleague, that, in our opinion, nothing would be more harmful for the Armenians that the agitation aroused by our adversaries for their egoistic political purposes in the peaceful and unfortunately neutral [American] press." Wangenheim's deputy made a personal visit to Morgenthau to show him Zimmerman's message and asked Morgenthau to issue an official denial of German involvement on behalf of the United States. Morgenthau refused; any statement would have to come from Washington. As Wangenheim's deputy departed, he admitted that the German ambassador was "not well at all".

On 21 October, Wangenheim had a stroke at supper. Two days later, Morgenthau received a phone call at 7.15 a.m. from the German Embassy. The German ambassador was dead. He had never recovered consciousness. Wangenheim's funeral was held two days later. The day before it had poured with rain, but the sun came out for his departure. Morgenthau wrote in his diary: "It was like a procession or death scene in a big opera. It was very well staged." The Turkish hierarchy turned out in all their finery, including the Grand Vizier. Together, they progressed to the elegant Dolmabahçe Palace on the waterside of the Bosphorus. Morgenthau fell into step with Enver and the pair talked about the war. At the end of the procession, Wangenheim's deputy, dressed in full uniform—including a helmet with a white plume—bid the American ambassador farewell as canons fired salvos in salute.

Four weeks later, Wangenheim's replacement arrived. Germany's new ambassador to Constantinople had been lured out of retirement. Paul Wolff Metternich was a German diplomat of the old school. Morgenthau noted after their first meeting,

> He is an aristocratic, very courtly gentleman, over six feet tall, looks you straight in your eyes, holds one's attentions closely, and is apparently a trifling hard of hearing and hides it by watching his companion closely and reading the lips. He is 62 years of age, a bachelor, and has been ambassador in Vienna, Paris and London. He told me he does not play bridge, cares little for clubs, and smokes only after lunch. He is very bright, has a splendid way of expressing himself and rounds his sentences off beautifully.

Metternich had already met the Grand Vizier, as well as Enver and Talaat, but was holding off his formal introduction to the Sultan, as the trunk containing his uniform

The Sultan's residence, Dolmabahçe Palace, taken between 1910 and 1915.

had not yet arrived. He was a stickler for tradition and anything else in life which he thought mattered; Turkish workmen were employed on a rush job to install a fireplace in his office at the German Embassy, as he refused to work without a live fire. His diplomatic experience, however, was quickly evident and he also paid far more attention to the demands from his consuls to protest about the Armenians to the Turkish government.

Less than a month after his arrival, he telegraphed the Chancellor:

I have seriously discussed the Armenian atrocities during the course of the past week with Enver [and others] ... They take refuge behind the plea of necessities of war, that revolutionaries need to be punished, and carefully evade the accusation that hundreds of thousands of women, children and elderly people are being driven into misery and ultimately to their deaths ... I presented my case in extremely sharp language. Protests are useless, and Turkish denials that no more deportations are to be undertaken are worthless.

Briefly, Morgenthau had found an ally. The Chancellor, however, had other ideas. The head of Germany's government had since the start of the genocide received details of what was going on from a reluctant Wangenheim and directly from Rössler and other consuls. Even Wangenheim had admitted to the Chancellor in summer 1915 that "the way in which the relocation [of Armenians] is being carried out shows that the government is indeed pursuing its purpose of eradicating the Armenian race from the Turkish Empire". Rössler had contacted the Chancellor repeatedly, while the Trebizond consul had pointed the finger directly at Talaat and Enver in mid-July: "I cannot help thinking that the Young Turkish Committee can be regarded as the driving force behind the measures being taken against the Armenians. The Central Committee seems to want to finally put an end to the Armenian question." The official line remained that Germany had done all it could to restrain the Turks, but from late autumn 1915, even the quiet protests in Constantinople were stopped. The Chancellor wrote in a note: "Our only aim is to keep Turkey on our side until the end of the war, no matter whether as a result the Armenians perish or not. If the war continues much longer we will need the Turks

Armenian refugees removing lice.

even more." The decision had been made, in the highest echelons of the German government, that genocide was an acceptable price to pay to win a war.

Two years and a day after Morgenthau had stepped off the train in Constantinople into a bustling and unfamiliar world, determined to represent his nation and its ideals on foreign soil, the American ambassador had become despondent. The weather was bad and he could not be bothered to get up.

> As it was raining pitchforks and it was dark in the morning, I remained in bed and had the barber shave me there. I was hardly finished with breakfast when Reshad Hikmet, [the Turkish] Under Secretary for Foreign Affairs, was announced ... He came to see me with a message ... to stop the American Consuls in Syria from busying themselves about Armenian affairs. He made the same argument that Enver has made so often, that the Armenians had made a great mistake in being disloyal during the war.

A few days later, as a cold snap set in and the rain turned to snow, he received an encouraging letter from the man who had sent him half way around the world. It read,

> My dear Mr. Ambassador: -
>   This is just a line to let you know that I am thinking of you and that I deeply and sincerely admire the way in which you are fulfilling the very trying obligations and duties of your present post. I have nothing special to write about, this is only a personal message to let you know that we are thinking of you constantly and that your labors are not passing unnoticed, but that we are very grateful.
> With warmest regards to Mrs. Morgenthau and yourself,
> Cordially and sincerely yours.

It was signed 'Woodrow Wilson'. In another set of circumstances, Morgenthau might have been encouraged, even galvanized by such a note from his president. But soon afterwards he wrote to his friend in the White House to ask to be given a leave of absence.

At the start of 1916, the American ambassador was still doing his best to help the Armenians, but it was difficult to get funds into the country. Morgenthau took it upon himself to pester the German banks in Constantinople—Deustche Orientbank and Deustche Bank—to see if they would allow him to wire money directly from

Armenian village women from Hawadorig, pre-1917, in deepest winter.

America, which would push down the exchange rate. He was, however, able to get $50,000 converted into Turkish pounds, which he began distributing to Red Cross hospitals treating the typhus outbreak. He even openly discussed with Metternich his method of surreptitiously sending the funds through his consuls and the German ambassador was sympathetic. Despite the official line of non-interference, Metternich had still spoken with Talaat, who had told him definitely that he would stop the deportations. Metternich bluntly admitted to Morgenthau he had already discovered that, when it came to the Armenians, Talaat and Enver were "not truthful in the matter".

Morgenthau was sat having tea with Metternich on 27 January 1916 when he received a telephone call notifying him that his request for a leave of absence had been granted. He began packing the following day. In his own mind, he was already determined not to return. He later wrote, "My failure to stop the destruction of the Armenians had made Turkey for me a place of horror, and I found intolerable my further association with men who, however gracious and accommodating and good-natured they might have been to the American ambassador, were still reeking with the blood of nearly a million human beings. Could I have done anything more ... I would willingly have stayed." On Saturday 29 January, he called on Talaat and Enver to say goodbye. For once, he did not mention the Armenians.

14. DER-EL-ZOR

From autumn 1915 onwards, the Armenian deportees who had survived the marches were forced on towards the desert. An indication of what was to come was given in a message from the German administrator in Aleppo: "Yesterday orders were given to clear town of deportees (20,000) within 14 days." He reported that he had been told, "300,000 are being sent into the South for 'resettlement' (Rakka, Der-el-Zor, Western Hauran). According to the aforesaid official, these are to be left to themselves at their destination and 'will all die' ... In any case, everything and anything is missing for relocation; neither tents, nor sufficient flour, nor fuel are being supplied to the concentration camps ... General conviction is that all deportees will meet their death." Having been evicted from their homes in the heat of summer—Jackson recorded that temperatures in Aleppo reached 46°C in July 1915—many refugees were once again on the road, this time in freezing winter weather. A German missionary from Aleppo reported, "In the cold of winter thousands of women, children, sick people have gone hungry and naked into the deserts and onto the roads." It snowed frequently and was so bitterly cold that sheets of ice were found in the Euphrates river.

The refugees' destination was a town called Der-el-Zor on the banks of the Euphrates, 200 miles east of Aleppo, at the edge of the desert. A German nun, whose community was trying to help the deportees, witnessed never-ending need. "The number of those pleading for help is endless ... The people are slaughtering and eating stray dogs ... One woman cut off her hair to sell it for bread. I saw how a woman ate the dried blood of a dead animal on the street. Up to now they all ate grass, but that has also dried up in the meantime." A captain in the German Medical Corps, who visited Der-el-Zor on route from Aleppo to Baghdad in late 1915 described the main camp there in a message to Rössler. "The entrance alone immediately displays the settlers' main occupation: burying the dead." At the time of the captain's visit, there were 30,000 people crammed into the town and camps nearby, with barely any food and no sanitation. "No linguistic expression of thought can even come close to describing the reality of this human misery." He added, "They are the forgotten whose only liberator is death."

Death was precisely the destination intended for the deportees, but the Turkish authorities' process of organized murder began further west. The first hints of what was coming came from Rössler, who telegrammed the German Embassy on 6 April 1916:

Mother and child.

"During the past few days, the Armenian concentration camp in Ras-ul-Ain was attacked by the Circassians and other similar people living nearby. The largest part of the unarmed 14,000 inmates was massacred. There are no further details at this point."

In early 1916, hundreds of thousands of those who had been deported were still alive, scattered in camps between Aleppo and Damascus and the Euphrates and Der-el-Zor. As winter turned to spring, hundreds of thousands were shunted farther along the deportation route and in early summer a new wave of carefully orchestrated massacres began. It was well underway by the time Metternich cabled the Chancellor in early July. He stated ominously, "The persecution of the Armenians in the eastern provinces has reached its final stage." He lamented that protestations from Western governments had achieved nothing at all. "The Turkish government has been put off in the execution of its programme for settling the Armenian question by destroying the Armenian race neither by our protests, nor by the protests of the American Embassy and the Papal Delegate, nor also by the threats of the Entente Powers, but least of all by considering the public opinion of the West. It is now about to dissolve and disperse the last groups of Armenians who have survived the deportations." He detailed the approach being taken: "The concentration camp at Rasul-Ain, which still had 2,000 inhabitants at the end of April, has been completely evacuated; a first transport has been attacked and smashed to pieces while walking towards Der [-el-] Zor; one can assume that the others have met no better fate." A few days later, Rössler passed on an update from Aleppo: "On 16 July, the news was received from Der-el-Zor that the Armenians had been ordered to continue their march ... After the Central Government had previously decreed that only as many Armenians were allowed to remain in Der-el-Zor as made up 10 percent of the total number of inhabitants, now the remainder were to be eradicated." On 15 April 1916, a convoy of Armenians left Der-el-Zor, with a small number reaching Mosul on 22 May. That summer, twenty-one further convoys were sent into the desert and not one survivor reached Mosul.

The Turkish authorities used death squads to murder Armenian deportees en masse once they had been marched a suitable distance away into the desert. One of the few Armenian eyewitness accounts of the process of extermination comes from Hosep Sarkissian, an Armenian labourer from Aintab who somehow survived. He recounted how all the deportees from Der-el-Zor and the surrounding area were put on the road in groups of between 2,000 and 4,000:

After travelling for several days, they camped on the banks of the Khabur River ... the next morning a band of Circassians on horseback came by and surrounded the caravans: they took everything away from them that they were still carrying and tore the clothes off their backs. The Circassians kept the money, jewellery, etc., and distributed the clothes among the Arabs who had appeared in crowds. Then the entire load, men, women, children, were driven naked for three hours until they reached a plateau on the north side of Karadagh surrounded by hills, where they were stopped. There, the Circassians threw themselves a second time into their victims, striking at the crown with axes, sabres, knives until blood flowed like a river and the entire plateau was covered in mutilated corpses.

Hosep hid himself under a pile of bodies. "Three days later, 31 people who were still alive crept out of their gruesome hiding places. For another three days they had to keep wandering without bread and water until they reached the Euphrates River."

Hosep's account did not reach Rössler in Aleppo until October, but by August, it was obvious what was happening. A German army officer sent in a report to the German Embassy on 29 August:

The road from Aleppo to Der-el-Zor (which the deportation convoys had been using for many months) now presents a different picture: it has become relatively quiet. It is true that at the stations closest to Aleppo there are still fairly large Armenian camps. But further to the south ... the camps are significantly reduced ... Der-el-Zor only has a few hundred craftsmen left who are working for the troops, whereas ... only 8 weeks ago many thousands ... were still in the camp ... The others had disappeared. The official version was that they had been sent onto Mosul ... but according to the general opinion of the people they had been murdered in the small valleys to the southeast of Der-el-Zor ... led away in groups a few hundred at a time and butchered to death by Circassians who had been especially commissioned to do so.

Jackson also began to hear stories of what was occurring and wrote in a personal letter to the chargé d'affaires who was the highest-ranking diplomat at the American Embassy following Morgenthau's departure:

I am reliably informed that the Mutessarif of Der-el-Zor has arranged and carried out the massacre of all the remaining Armenians that were there, some

12,000 in all ... There have been a number of persons arrested at [Der-el] Zor for having distributed relief, some beaten to death, and some hung really for that reason but said to be for others ... I may tell you that I do not like the situation here at all, and believe it possible that if the Turks see the end near they will do every Christian in the country, in which event my head would not be worth a cent.

The scale of what was going on was far beyond the 12,000 Jackson was made aware of. From July to December 1916, it has been assessed that 192,750 people were slaughtered at Der-el-Zor.

Large swathes of eastern Turkey were now a giant Armenian ghost town. Where their homes had not been appropriated by Muslims, empty houses stood in silent sentinel to the departed. The western regions where Armenians lived had also been completely depopulated. A German traveller there wrote,

Almost all of the Armenians from this area have disappeared. Entire villages are uninhabited. Some of the houses have been sealed, but they are completely empty. Furniture and similar objects [are] stored in depots, but seem to disappear from there. The Armenian quarter in Ismid was burned down ... Adapazar is almost completely deserted; almost all the stores are closed. Craftsmen, shoemakers, tailors, etc., are missing. Almost all the towns must do without doctors, pharmacists, etc. The silk industry, particularly in the area around Geive, has been completely suspended; the spinning mills are closed.

The picture was worse in the east. Scheubner-Richter, the German administrator in Erzerum, reported, "On the journey from Erzerum to Mosul via Khinis, Mush, Bitlis and Sairt, all the villages and homes I came across, all of which used to be inhabited by Armenians, were found to be totally empty and destroyed."

Metternich refused to keep quiet and continued to raise the treatment of the Armenians with Talaat and Enver. When the Turkish Foreign Minister visited Berlin in summer 1916, he complained that Metternich had "offended" the Turkish government with his frequent interventions. The seasoned diplomat, who had been ambassador in multiple European capitals, had done no more than Morgenthau, in fact much less, but he was refusing to toe the line. On 3 October 1916, after less than eleven months in post, Metternich was recalled. Even Zimmerman, now

The bleached bones of Armenians massacred near Erzerum.

that the slaughter taking place at Der-el-Zor was irrefutable, could not condone it. The day before Metternich was summoned back to Berlin, Zimmermann cabled the German Embassy that he had spoken to the Turkish Foreign Minister and told him, "The measures now planned against the sad remains of the Armenians, consisting of women and children, could in no way be justified or excused. The actions of the Turkish government will cause a storm of indignation throughout the entire civilized world, which will not even die down soon after the war." As Metternich journeyed home in disgrace, the chargé d'affaires representing Germany in his stead messaged the Chancellor that of the two million Armenians previously in Turkey, one and half million had been deported. Of those deported, more than a million were thought to be dead.

15. THE CURTAIN CLOSES

On 6 April 1917, the United States entered the war on the side of the Allies. Turkey immediately severed diplomatic relations and Leslie Davis, like almost all the other American diplomats, burned all copies of his reports on the genocide, in accordance with the instructions he received from the Embassy. He was not asked to leave immediately, but the local police chief did pay him a visit to demand he take down the American flag which normally fluttered above the Consulate. He finally departed on 16 May 1917 and rode the nearly 500 miles to reach the railroad to Constantinople. Along with all the other American diplomats, he then returned home.

Armenians still survived in pockets largely in what is now Syria: 60,000 in Damascus, 30,000 in Homs and Hama and around 45,000 women and children in Aleppo. Some Armenian men were still working on railways or in labour battalions, but many of them were rounded up and murdered as the year progressed. The organized campaign of murder against the Armenians was largely stopped in 1917, simply because there were so few of them left within Turkey.

Talaat had now ascended from the position of Minister of the Interior to that of Grand Vizier, the CUP using the war to cement its control of Turkish politics. The day after becoming head of the government, Talaat delivered a public address. Typically, it rewrote history in Turkey's favour. "The Russian naval attack in the Black Sea and the land-based attack on our borders forced us to embrace the party toward which our historical destiny was carrying us and take our place alongside the Great Powers." The fact that the Turkish navy had attacked the Russians in the Black Sea first was simply air-brushed from the record. He went on to address the Armenian question: "Our enemies everywhere are saying that we ... have committed all sorts of atrocities against the Armenians ... Fortunately, however, many people in different places are beginning to understand the invidious, pernicious nature of these reports." He then went on to trot out the familiar lines about Van, the Armenian connection with Russia and the threat to the army: "We proceeded to carry out deportations for the good of the army. We cannot claim that this deportation took place under normal conditions ... since most of the gendarmes had been incorporated into the army. The central government however ... brought all those who had committed acts of violence before court martial." Far from having created, organized and armed the *chetes*, the party line was now that their actions were an unfortunate overreach, a statement which also ignores the direct involvement of the Turkish military in the entire operation to exterminate the Armenians. Talaat concluded by stating, "Every government has the right to defend itself against those who stage armed revolts."

Germany's new ambassador in Turkey, who was eyeing promotion and whose opinions were generally carefully choreographed to align with those of his superiors, did admit to the Chancellor; "the extermination policy has damaged the Turkish state. The atrocities of the Armenian campaigns will weigh heavily on the Turkish name for a long time to come ... Internally, the country has been noticeably weakened by the downfall and banishment of a physically strong, hard-working and thrifty people."

In May 1917, the German consul in Aleppo again got in touch with the Chancellor. A German engineer, probably one of the many working on the railways for the Turks, had stumbled across a mass grave near Der-el-Zor. Rössler wrote,

I respectfully enclose for Your Excellency's kind attention a memorandum by Mr. Bunte, a certified engineer, on observations made during the journey along the River Khabur from 1 to 6 April [1917]. There is no doubt that large numbers of human skulls and bones to be found there are from the Armenian massacres which took place the previous July and August [1916]. Bunte, said he "found a large number of bleached human skulls and skeletons ... some of the skulls had bullet holes ... The population spoke of 12,000 Armenians who were massacred, shot or drowned here alone".

A few days later, a German member of parliament brought up the issue of the Armenians in the chamber of the Reichstag. The Social Democrat, Georg Ledebour, had already raised the issue in September 1916 and Zimmermann had managed to head off debate. In a private meeting, he told colleagues:

To my utmost regret, the member of the Reichstag, [Georg] Ledebour has today brought up the Armenian question again. Gentlemen, you all know with what clever means of distortion and exaggeration our enemies have exploited this issue to instigate a slanderous campaign against us and our Turkish ally ... As regards the reasons and the course of events which we, too, deeply lament ... It is our enemies themselves who are mainly to blame

Skulls of deportees.

for the tragedy of the Armenian people. Long before the outbreak of the war, through unscrupulous agitation, they stirred up the Armenians against the Turkish government.

Whether Zimmermann, who had now secured promotion to Secretary of State, believed his own lie is hard to assess; perhaps he had repeated the Turkish propaganda so often that he had convinced himself. He offered to discuss the Armenians with Ledebour and other members, but only in a private, closed session.

The Russian threat, which had for so long occupied the Turkish government, was now disintegrating. Unrest and pressure from the army forced the abdication of the Tsar as soldiers in the Russian army deserted in droves. Finally, in October 1917, the Red Guards stormed the historical St Petersburg residence of the Russian monarchy. Lenin immediately declared an armistice. All the territory which the Turks had lost to the Russians was about to be regained. However, as one threat receded, another came sharply into focus. In December 1917, a British army which had set out from Egypt captured Jerusalem.

By spring 1918, the Germans were already thinking about the end of the war. As the General Staff compiled plans for a great new offensive on the Western

Front, with Russia out of the equation, a German victory was still seen in some quarters as a very real possibility. But the Foreign Office was already anticipating that the Armenian question would crop up in any post-war negotiation. In March 1918, Zimmermann's deputy at the German Foreign Office messaged the Embassy in Constantinople: "In future peace negotiations with the Western allies these will without doubt bring up the Armenian issue and try to enforce as extensive autonomy as possible for the East Anatolian *vilayets*. In the face of such attempts, the position of Turkey will be much more favourable if it has presented tangible evidence before entering the negotiation that it intends to provide the Christian as well as Muslim citizens of this province with equal, mild and fair treatment." He proposed the resettlement and "speedy return" of Armenians, ending, "I request ... in your talks with the Grand Vizier, with the Minister of Foreign Affairs and also with Enver Pasha, to develop this concept and to report on their response to your ideas." It was a laughable notion, but one the Embassy was duty bound to explore. The reply two weeks later was abrupt. Arranging any resettlement was proving difficult, it explained, because the Turks were being "clumsy and slow". What was

Starving Armenian children.

more relevant was that as early as September 1915, the Turkish Government had officially appropriated all Armenian-owned property and assets, even going as far as to try and get Armenian money out of American banks, although Morgenthau had quickly put a stop to the idea. Although many Armenian villages were deserted they had frequently also been looted and destroyed and where homes did still exist, many had been taken by local Muslims, or in some cases refugees who had been resettled by the government. In reality, even if Armenians had wanted to return, there were very few places they could go back to. Very understandably, they also did not want to. As the German Embassy admitted to the Foreign Office, the other reason the notion of resettlement was ludicrous was that "All of the Armenians were already scared to death."

That month, as the Russian army fell apart, Turkish soldiers reclaimed Erzerum, Van and then a few weeks after the Persian region of Urmia. The advance into Urmia led to a mass exodus of Assyrians. Attacked by bands of Kurds, 70,000 travelled across Iran to reach Hamadan, which was under the control of the British. A British lieutenant later witnessed the carnage: "all along the main road taken by the wretches lay a terrifying number of bodies, men, women, and children, who had been stripped by the Kurds; flocks of crows covered the corpses." Only around 50,000 made it to safety. But as the Turks marched triumphantly east, the tide of the war finally turned against Germany in the west. Turkey would win its age-old battle against Russia, but it was going to lose the war.

On 30 September 1918, Damascus fell to the British. An Armenian survivor of the death marches, who had reached safety elsewhere in Syria, wrote in his diary when he heard the news, "Three days ago, the British army occupied Damascus. The criminal, arrogant soldiers ... who have bullied us so much, are now miles away from us and there is no possibility they will return and recapture the territory they have lost. The swords of the cursed irregular bands [the *chetes*] can no longer reach us. We are as happy as if we had been reborn!" Three and a half weeks later, British and Indian cavalry, accompanied by armoured cars, rode into the city of Aleppo as smoke from the torched railway station billowed upward, darkening the sky. Ahead of the cavalry, 12,000 Turks retreated northward. A Melbourne newspaper broadcast the news to its Australian readers three days later under the headline, "Aleppo taken by British dashing cavalry feat." The soldiers rescued 125,000 Armenian survivors from the desert. Four days later, Turkey signed an armistice with the Allies. Among many other clauses, the Treaty of Mudros, as the armistice agreement was known, granted the release of all those who had been

Armenian refugees receiving food relief from the American Committee for Relief in the Near East, 1916.

interned and permitted the Armenian deportees to return home. It was signed by the Minister of the Navy, as the CUP leadership was too preoccupied with escaping. Talaat and Enver slipped away to Odessa aboard a German submarine on the night of 3 November, from where Talaat travelled to Berlin and Enver fled to the Caucasus. Officially, the war was over and the Armenians were safe. A few days before Talaat's departure, he confided in a Turkish war hero, showing some apparent sign of remorse, even though he was the main architect of the genocide. "I find it unconscionable to blame me and other high ranking government officials of having failed to prevent these atrocities ... I confess I am deeply saddened and pained that we failed to prevent the murder of these Armenians who had no involvement in rebellious activities." Once again, Talaat was trying to rewrite history, this time in his own mind.

16. ON TRIAL

Turkey still had its own government, but British soldiers marched the streets of Constantinople. The instincts of the German Foreign Office had been correct: the Allies had not forgotten what Turkey had done to the Armenians. Under pressure from Britain, the Sultan agreed to put the CUP leaders on trial. Feeling still ran high in the United States too. The head of an American fact-finding mission sent to the former Ottoman Empire after the war concluded, "Mutilation, violation, torture and death have left their haunting memories in a hundred beautiful Armenian valleys ... evidence of the most colossal crime of all the ages." In the unencumbered view of the British Prime Minister, David Lloyd George, the Turks were "a human cancer ... [with] a long record of infamy against humanity".

The notion of trying those responsible for actions during war time was comparatively new. A group of countries had agreed the Hague Convention at conferences in 1899 and 1907, which attempted to put limits on how war could be conducted, although it had been frequently ignored; one of the articles of the convention forbade the use of "asphyxiating gases", while another the dropping of explosives from balloons. Both sides in the First World War used poisoned gas and dropped bombs from aircraft. Crucially, the convention also covered what were defined as the "laws of humanity" which it was decided Turkey had transgressed. The result was the first war crimes trials of the twentieth century.

From January 1919, many of the CUP leaders who were left, along with war-time cabinet ministers, provincial governors and some military officers, were reluctantly rounded up. Some were released by Turkish authorities and the British took the unprecedented step of detaining a number of party leaders and imprisoning them on the Mediterranean island of Malta. On 12 February 1919, *The New York Times* informed its readers, "The trial of those responsible for the Armenian massacres by the Turks has begun in Constantinople ... The prosecutor, in opening the trial, said it was necessary to punish the authors of the massacres which had filled the whole world with a feeling of horror."

The trials were held in the Grand Hall of the Ministry of Justice in Constantinople and each day's events published in the Constantinople newspapers. The defendants were classified as either 'principal co-perpetrators' or 'accessories' to crimes under the

Forty slaughtered Armenians, a picture obtained by the American Red Cross in February 1919, showing that massacres continued even after the armistice.

Ottoman penal code including 'deportation and massacre'. Among those who testified were Muslim leaders from various districts and Armenian survivors. The court did see many incriminating documents, including twelve coded telegrams giving direct orders for the deportations, which officials admitted were instructions to massacre the Armenian population. However, many other documents were found to be 'missing'. Despite this, the evidence was sufficiently incriminating. Talaat and Enver were found guilty of 'first degree mass murder' and condemned to death in absentia, while the governors of Urfa and Yozgat were publicly executed. Resid Bey, the sadistic *vali* of Diyarbakir, shot himself through the head rather than face the noose.

From the start, the trials were largely unpopular within Turkey. The funeral of the governor of Yozgat became a rally, where protestors chanted anti-British slogans and then laid wreaths with the inscription that he was a "great martyr for the Turks". A fund for his family raised 20,000 Turkish pounds. It was an early sign that Allied hopes for a neat post-war settlement in which Turkey accepted its responsibility in defeat, were to be dashed. If nothing else, the military commitment to bring the former Ottoman Empire to heel was staggering. The British had taken control of the Dardanelles Straits and stationed soldiers in Constantinople, while the French were in Cilicia as they were preparing to take control of Syria, but elsewhere in Turkey there were pockets of resistance and whole regions that were effectively lawless.

In early 1920, the rising nationalist sentiment in Turkey finally boiled over. The man responsible was Mustafa Kemal Ataturk, the only Turkish general to be undefeated in the First World War. Tasked with re-organizing the post-war Ottoman army in 1919, he had instead tried to organize an uprising against the British and then gathered together a group of likeminded followers. Support for the movement spread so fast that nationalists—under the banner of the 'Defence of National Rights' movement—secured victory in parliamentary elections.

In late January 1920, Ataturk's forces laid siege to the city of Marash in eastern Turkey, which was garrisoned by 2,000 French soldiers. The city was also home to 20,000 repatriated Armenians, who had returned to the city the year before. After three weeks, despite having been reinforced, the French were ordered to withdraw. They tried to do so under cover of darkness to avoid panicking the local population, but several thousand attempted to follow. The initial reports suggested that Armenians had died when a snow blizzard engulfed the fleeing refugees, but the truth was far more sinister. The Turkish nationalist forces had perpetrated a massacre. On 28 February, *The Times* correspondent reported, "the French had evacuated Marash, and three thousand Armenians were massacred while attempting to escape ... Great numbers were frozen to death during the flight. Twenty thousand remained at Marash, of whom sixteen thousand were massacred." An American missionary doctor despairingly wrote, "Returning from that exile and beginning with energy to live once more and to hope once more, they find themselves betrayed, and that by their allies, massacred by their conquered enemy, and stripped barer than they were in 1915 ... Where can we appeal? ... Are we to see this tragedy carried out to completion before our very eyes?" The British Foreign Secretary was outraged and telegrammed the High Commissioner in Constantinople:

The information as to Armenian massacres ... whether the figures be or not exaggerated—is so serious that the Allied Governments, who are in complete agreement on the matter, are compelled to take urgent action ... some drastic measure should be taken, and this might assume the form of occupying the War Office or some important Government building, and of securing the persons of the Grand Vizier and the Minister of War ... and placing them in confinement.

Turkish nationalists were threatening Armenian populations across eastern Turkey. The French had come to an agreement with Ataturk to halt further attacks, which theoretically included protection for Armenians. When the French prepared to pull out of Aintab in June, they offered to transport the 15,000 Armenians who had resettled there thirty miles south, to the Syrian border town of Kilis for their protection. The outraged Armenians determined that instead of being deported again they would stay and defend themselves, prompting Jackson, who was still American consul in Aleppo, to report, "Unless the world is to hear of one of the worst horrors in its history within fifteen or twenty days at the utmost something drastic must be done at once to save the situation. Fifteen thousand souls will surely perish in the most blood curdling terrifying manner if these people are turned over to the Turks." The result was a year-long siege, although in the end there was no massacre at Aintab. Armenians who had returned home to other towns were not so fortunate. They were prevented from opening shops or working in fields, denied the right to reclaim properties, or worse. A few months later, the U.S. State Department was glibly informed, "A report received through the American mission sources from Adana indicates confirmation of the destruction of [Hadjin] ... by the Turks and the massacre of nearly [the] entire Armenian population of eight thousand." A French missionary described what was going on in the areas of Cilicia under nationalist control as "Systematic plunder and extermination of Christians". The Turkish nationalists, while not attempting the organized eradication of the Armenians in the manner of Talaat's government, were determined not to let them resettle in Turkey and, if they remained, were perfectly comfortable with murdering them.

As the uprising escalated, the new nationalist Turkish parliament voted itself in line with Ataturk's ambitions. The central claim was that all the areas that had not been physically occupied by the Allies at the moment of the armistice remained the Turkish homeland. The Sultan, increasingly a puppet of the British, shut down the chamber and the British imposed martial law in Constantinople. In response, Ataturk set up a rival government in Ankara and began making overtures to the Soviet government in Moscow. The supposedly simple peace was unravelling and Armenians were still being slaughtered.

17. THE END OF ARMENIA

Charities were still raising vast sums for displaced Armenians. Morgenthau, now Vice Chair of the American Committee for Armenian and Syrian Relief, which had been renamed again, to the more pithy Near East Relief, continued to campaign for aid.

1917 appeal poster from the American Committee for Relief in the Near East.

Posters were put up across thousands of billboards across the country, urging Americans to aid the starving Armenians because "Hunger knows no armistice".

Henry Morgenthau wrote in one newspaper, "Two hundred and fifty thousand children, orphaned by the unspeakable Turks, are calling in the only English they know, 'Bread, Uncle Sam.'" He asserted that the survivors and the Armenian diaspora should be protected. "These peoples must be freed from the agony and danger of such horrors. They must not only be saved for the present but either thru governmental action or protection under the League of Nations they must be given assurance that they will be free in peace and that no harm can come to them." The newly formed League of Nations was President Wilson's great world peace project, intended to mean that nation would never fight against nation again. The solution to the Armenian question seemed simple: create a sovereign, independent Armenia. It was, as noted by the League of Nations governing council itself, "an object which will receive, and which will deserve to receive, the sympathy and support of enlightened opinion

Poster from the special campaign of the American Committee for Armenian and Syrian Relief (renamed by 1916 the American Committee for Relief in the Near East) throughout the war to raise funds and provide relief. (Cornell University)

throughout the civilized world". Sadly, enlightened opinion was to prove insufficient when what was needed was armed men and money.

The proposed borders of the new Armenia were still not yet defined, but it was already decided that much of Anatolia, which included the towns of Erzerum, Diyarbakir, Harput and Van, would probably be included. The plan was effectively to partition Turkey and create a new state of Armenia out of regions in the Caucasus and what had previously been eastern Turkey. The problem was that while a nation could be born on paper, it would not exist on the ground for long if it could not maintain the integrity of its borders. The Turkish parliament, until it had been dissolved, had unequivocally asserted its opposition to any such notion. Meanwhile, none of the Allied governments wanted to volunteer their armies to police the new state and the League of Nations had no men at arms on which it could call to enforce its noble ideals. President Wilson tried to propose that Armenia become a U.S. mandate under the League of Nations, with the support of Morgenthau, who wrote in *The New York Times*, "I am aware that this proposition is not popular with the American people. But it seems to me to be a matter

Armenian refugee children in Gyumri, Armenia, circa 1919.

in which we do not have a choice ... if the Greeks, the Syrians, the Armenians ... are not freed from the most revolting tyranny that history has ever known, we shall understand that all the sacrifices of the last four years have been in vain, and that the much-discussed new ideals in the government of the world are the merest cant." His efforts and the efforts of the President were to no avail and political opposition quashed the idea of a United States mandate for Armenia. Philanthropy was one thing, intertwining U.S. interests with a small nation which, in the words of one Republican senator, was a "poorhouse" with nothing to offer, was a very different prospect, especially in an election year. Despite the fact that it would have no ability to secure its own borders, plans to draw up a new Armenian state continued to be worked out anyway.

In August 1920, the Constantinople government signed the Treaty of Sèvres with the Allies. With the stroke of a pen, the Ottoman Empire was formally ended and an independent Armenia created. The Armenian nation had already been officially recognized by the Allies and by the United States; by a quirk of international diplomacy, the country's existence had been accepted before its borders had been defined.

British troops march by the Nusretiye mosque.

President Wilson was landed with the task of drawing the lines on the map, creating an Armenian state with a territory of over 26,000 square miles. But the President's marks on the map were irrelevant. In November 1920, the new-born state of Armenia was invaded by Turkish nationalist forces from the west and Soviet troops from the east; a few months later the Soviets signed a treaty with Ataturk, recognizing Turkey, as defined by the nationalists, and also secretly agreeing to supply and arm thousands of nationalist soldiers. The British Prime Minister blamed the League of Nations for not protecting Armenia, but the British were already shying away from the prospect of another war. The prisoners held on Malta were released, in exchange for British soldiers who had been kidnapped by nationalists, and the war crimes trials were quietly dropped. In January 1921 they were officially abolished. In the face of the prevailing wind, the British agreed to negotiate a new settlement for post-war Turkey.

Armenian children, probably orphans, found begging in Ekaterinodar, southern Russia, in 1919.

In November 1922, representatives of the Allied governments, along with the U.S. and Turkey gathered at the picturesque Swiss lakeside town of Lausanne. The Turkish delegation was adamant from the outset that any discussion of Armenians was off the table, even threatening to shut down the talks. At the end of the war, the Turkish government had had little choice but to accept whatever conditions the Allies wished to impose. Four years later, the Allies were keen to bring their troops home and the Americans were keen to secure a future deal over trade and oil. The U.S. ambassador in Switzerland wrote in his diary, "there is no subject upon which the Turks are more fixed in obstinacy [than the Armenians]." *The New York Times*

Mustafa Kemal Ataturk.

reported that the Armenians, who sent a delegation to the conference, who the Turks refused to listen to, had been "thrown overboard". The following year, the Allies and Turkey signed the Treaty of Lausanne, agreeing the recognition of a sovereign Republic of Turkey. The treaty stated, "The Turkish Government undertakes to assure full and complete protection of life and liberty to all inhabitants of Turkey without distinction of birth, nationality, language, race or religion." The Turkish negotiators had even managed to secure an agreement that the text would not even mention the Armenians by name. In March 1923, months before the treaty was signed, Ataturk decreed a general amnesty for all who had been convicted in the war crimes trials.

A few weeks before British soldiers liberated tens of thousands of emaciated survivors from camps in the desert outside Aleppo in 1918, the diplomat who had tried to halt the genocide and campaigned tirelessly to aid the survivors, wrote a passionate plea in the Red Cross magazine. "Will the outrageous terrorizing, the cruel torturing, the driving of women into harems. the debauchery of innocent girls, the sale of many of them at eighty cents each, the murdering of hundreds of thousands, the destruction of hundreds of villages and cities—will the wilful execution of this whole devilish scheme to annihilate the Armenian, Greek and [As]Syrian Christians of Turkey, will all this go unpunished?" Almost exactly five years later, Henry Morgenthau had his answer.

EPILOGUE

The war crimes trials of those responsible for organizing and carrying out the massacre of over a million Armenians never resumed. But there was a reckoning for Talaat. On 15 March 1921, he was walking down a street in a western suburb of Berlin, when a young man came up behind him. After confirming Talaat's identity, Soghomon Tehlirian, a twenty-five-year-old Armenian student, shot Talaat through the head at point-blank range with a pistol. It was his plan all along to be arrested. To make sure its readers connected the dots, *The New York Times* ran the sub-heading: "Armenian Student Shoots Former Turkish Grand Vizier, Held Responsible for Massacres". Tehlirian was from Erzinjan, a town a hundred miles east of Erzerum. His mother and three sisters and brothers had perished

Soghomon Tehlirian.

in the genocide, along with eighty-five members of his extended family. The murder of Talaat was, for him, an assassination.

Tehlirian's trial opened shortly afterwards. Under German law, he was charged with murder. Instead of pleading his innocence, he intended to bring to light Talaat's actions in the genocide and the German government's knowledge of them. The defence openly accepted that he had shot Talaat, but focused instead on Tehlirian's mental state and his conviction that Talaat was the main author of the genocide. In effect, they argued that the murder was justly motivated, utilizing to the full Tehlirian's story, in which he described being deported and later returning to his home town to find his family house in ruins. Remarkably, the strategy worked. The former German consul in Aleppo, Walter Rössler, was among those called to testify. He wrote to the German Foreign Office:

> If the German Foreign Office should give its permission that I be examined as a witness in the proceedings against the murderer of Talaat Pasha, I would have to be released from the official secrecy and would be obliged to answer all of the presiding judge's questions under the oath I would swear as a witness. I would not be able to avoid expressing my conviction that Talaat Pasha is, in fact, one of those Turkish statesmen who wanted the Armenians to be annihilated and carried this out according to plan.

Unsurprisingly, the Foreign Office refused him permission to appear at the trial for anything other than to be examined on "pure facts" and then banned him from appearing at all. Even though Rössler could be silenced, Talaat's role in the genocide and the German government's full knowledge of events became public and was splashed across the front pages of the German press, where it was read by a deeply shocked public. Tehlirian's own account disturbed those listening in

The memorial chapel to the Armenian Genocide in Margadeh in the Syrian desert. (Ashnag)

court. He told how he had been deported with his family, seen his young sister raped and his brother's head cleaved open with an axe. He himself was struck on the head and left for dead, but regained consciousness to find he was buried beneath a pile of bodies. Despite clear instructions from the judge that any position on the justification for Talaat's killing was not within their remit, and that they were only to take into account "whether or not the defendant knew that he was killing an individual and that he wanted to kill him", the German twelve-man jury acquitted Tehlirian. It only took them an hour's deliberation to find him not guilty of murder.

Enver did not meet an assassin's bullet, but instead died opposing Ataturk's nationalists by fighting against the Soviet advance in the Caucasus, defending Ottoman-Turkey against the old enemy. According to some accounts, he was killed leading a cavalry charge into machine-gun fire.

Henry Morgenthau acted as Vice Chair for the Near East Relief charity and assisted President Wilson at the Versailles post-war treaty deliberations in Paris. He had hoped his friend would run for a third term, but the Democrat Party were unenthused about selecting a now gravely ill and increasingly unpopular man as their presidential candidate. Tired of Wilson's war and messianic ambition to change the world, the American electorate shied away from the Democrats and voted in a Republican isolationist as president in 1920. By the time the Allies agreed the Treaty of Lausanne with Turkey, obliterating all hope of an independent Armenia, the occupant of the White House no longer cared. For the rest of his life, Morgenthau ably assisted multiple charities working in the Middle East, before passing away in New York at the age of ninety. He died in 1946, just as the war crimes trials of the Nazis who had orchestrated the murder of millions of Morgenthau's own race, the Jews, came to a conclusion at Nuremberg.

Historians have drawn many parallels between Hitler's holocaust and what happened to the Armenians. There is no doubt, given the Führer's statement prior to the invasion of Poland, that he was fully aware that a nation's war-time moralizing could be easily overcome by post-conflict realpolitik. Whether the orchestrators of the Holocaust copied elements of the Turkish genocide method is harder to prove, but not beyond the realms of possibility; the first pictures the world saw of desperate women and children peering through the slit-doors of cattle trucks and naked bodies piled up in ditches were of Armenians. At the most basic level, the Armenian Genocide and the Holocaust both demonstrate the consequences of human beings' ability to dehumanize; in the case of the Jews because of their race, in the case of the Armenians, Assyrians and Greeks on the basis of their race and religion. There are parallels also between those who deny the existence of both genocides. It is remarkable how the apparently incontrovertible, when inconvenient, becomes seemingly refutable. Richard Cohen, a *Washington Post* correspondent, had that very experience:

> I found myself sitting at the end of an enormous table in the embassy of Turkey. At the other end was the ambassador himself and what he was telling me was that the crime I had always thought had happened had not ... [and] what the world persisted in calling genocide was actually a civil war—one with atrocities on both sides and one in which the Central Government in Constantinople lost control over its own troops and could not protect the Armenians ... Sure, there were 'incidents' and, yes, the Armenians had been banished ... And so I sat there at the table unable to prove that one of the great crimes of history had actually been committed.

An independent Armenia has existed since the fall of the Soviet Union. But even cordial diplomatic relations with Turkey have been prevented by the Turkish government's failure to admit the genocide ever took place. In 2004, the United States Consul General in Istanbul, David Arnett, sent a confidential message to Washington. The note, entitled 'Armenian "Genocide" and the Ottoman archives' was subsequently made public via a Wikileaks hack. Arnett stated, "The most significant obstacle to Turkish-Armenian reconciliation remains a lack of agreement or even healthy dialogue on the Armenian 'question' or what most Turks refer to as the 'supposed genocide'." He added that while Armenian scholars claim 1.5 million Armenians were killed, modern Turkish historians argue no more than a few hundred thousand Armenians perished because of bandits, disease and harsh conditions. There is also evidence to suggest that the Ottoman archives were conveniently purged of incriminating documents in the 1980s, before being partially opened up to researchers. Arnett's originally secret message notes:

> From the inception of the Republic, Ataturk and his establishment heirs have asserted that maintenance of a 'Turkish identity'—which Ataturk and his circle developed as an artificial construct and which his political heirs claim is under threat from domestic and foreign enemies—is essential to the preservation and development of the Republic. Representatives of both the Turkish state and every government to date believe that acknowledging any wrongs inflicted on the Armenians would call into question Turkey's own claims of victimization and its borders.

Armenian Genocide memorial, Yerevan.

There has been no justice and no truth and reconciliation commission for those who survived the horrors that took place between 1915 and 1917.

On a hill, overlooking the centre of the Armenian capital of Yerevan, sits a monument to the victims of the genocide. The centrepiece is a permanently lit flame, surrounded by twelve stones, representing the twelve Armenian provinces 'lost' to modern-day Turkey. Nearby is a 100-metre-long basalt wall, on which are carved the names of every population that was massacred. There is no list of individual names, simply because so many are unknown.

At the end of wall, as you near the flame, are glass cases containing soil from the graves of political and intellectual figures who spoke out against the genocide, among them Henry Morgenthau. In death, as in life, he stands with the Armenians, victims of the first genocide of the twentieth century.

ANNOTATED SELECT BIBLIOGRAPHY

The sources for quotes found in this book have been included in the following bibliography, along with a selection of books by other authors referenced in the writing of this work. I have also included a number of works which cover in depth areas which have only been touched upon briefly and may be of further interest to some readers.

PRIMARY SOURCES RELATING TO AMBASSADOR HENRY MORGENTHAU AND OTHER DIPLOMATS

Henry Morgenthau, at the urging of President Wilson, published his own account of the Armenian Genocide in 1918, entitled *Ambassador Morgenthau's Story*. He also later wrote an autobiographical work, which encompassed his time in Turkey. His personal diaries from his time as ambassador have been collated by Ara Sarafian. In the few instances where there are slightly varying accounts of events, I have opted for Morgenthau's diaries as the likely more authoritative source, given their contemporary nature:

Morgenthau, Henry, ed. Sarafian, Ara, *United States Diplomacy on The Bosphorus: The Diaries of Ambassador Morgenthau 1913–1916*, Taderon Press, 2004

Morgenthau, Henry, *Ambassador Morgenthau's Story*, Doubleday, 1918

_____, *All in a Lifetime*, Doubleday, Page & Company, 1922

The reports of Leslie Davis, the United States' consul in Harput, were published in 1988:

Davis, Leslie A., Aristide D (ed.). *The Slaughterhouse Province: An American Diplomat's Report on the Armenian Genocide of 1915–1917*, Caratzas, 1988

Ara Sarafian's work to compile a record of relevant communications from U.S. official records is one the most invaluable contemporaneous resources on the genocide. The documents from U.S. archives include telegrams from Morgenthau and his colleagues to Washington, to which they frequently attached the eyewitness accounts of American missionaries and others:

Sarafian, Ara (ed.), *United States Official Records on The Armenian Genocide 1915–1917*, Taderon Press, 2004

English translations of the records from the German Foreign Office archives have been helpfully put together by Wolfgang Gust. The remarkable collection sheds light on the varying attitudes to the genocide of different German diplomats. The urgent protestations of Rössler, the Aleppo consul, clearly refute the overly simplistic claim that German diplomats simply stood by and watched, or aided and abetted the Turkish authorities in their programme of murder. As with the records from the U.S. Foreign Office, they also include eyewitness testimonies, usually from Rössler and the other consuls, which were frequently sent directly to the German Chancellor himself. Wangeheim's aloof attitude to the treatment of the Armenians is clearly evident in the tone of his own communication. Overall, the archival evidence unequivocally demonstrates that those at the very top of the German government were fully aware of the extent of the genocide. They also had the best access to information, as German diplomats were the only ones permitted to communicate using cipher following the outbreak of the First World War:

Gust, Wolfgang (ed.), *The Armenian Genocide: Evidence from the German Foreign Office Archives, 1915–1916*, Berghahn Books, 2013

An account of the lead-up to the genocide and the genocide itself can be found in the following works:

Johannes Østrup, Erindringer, quoted in Bjørnlund, Matthias, *'When the Cannons Talk, the Diplomats Must Be Silent': A Danish Diplomat in Constantinople during the Armenian Genocide*, Genocide Studies and prevention, Issue 2, Article 8, International Association of Genocide Scholars, 2006

OTHER EYEWITNESS ACCOUNTS OF THE GENOCIDE AND PRIMARY SOURCES

Arguably one of the single most powerful collection of eyewitness accounts of the genocide is that compiled by the Viscount Bryce and the historian Arnold J. Tynbee. Bryce brought up the treatment of the Armenians in the House of Lords and recruited a young history graduate, who would later go on to become a renowned historian, to put together annotated, eyewitness testimonies of the genocide while it was still underway in 1916. The original version of the 'Blue Book' was published with many names redacted or altered. However, it has since been published multiple times, and is now available in full and uncensored. It is also available in its original form in the British National Archives, along with additional correspondence. (See collection FO 96/205.)

Chitjian, Mardiros, Hamzarpartoum, 'A Hair's breadth from death: the memoirs of Hamzarpartoum, Mardiros, Chitjian', Taderon Press, 2003

Dadrian, Vahram, *To the Desert: Pages From my Diary*, Taderon Press, 2003

Miller, Donald E. & Miller, Lorna Touryan, *Survivors: An Oral history of the Armenian Genocide*, University of California Press, 1993

Rafael Nogales was a Venezuelan mercenary who fought on the Ottoman Caucasus front in the First World War. He tried to intervene to stop the massacre of Armenians in the town of Aldicevaz, near Van, in April 1915:

Nogales, Rafael de, translated Lee, Muna, *Four Years Beneath the Crescent*, Taderon Press, 2003

Odian, Yervan, *Accursed Years: My Exile and Return From Der Zor, 1914–1919*, Garod Books Ltd, 2009

Sarafian, Ara & Avenbury, Eric, *British Parliamentary Debates on the Armenian Genocide, 1915–1918*, Taderon Press, 2003

Sarafian, Ara, *Talaat Pasha's Report on the Armenian Genocide, 1917*, Taderon Press, 2011

Toynbee, Arnold, *The Treatment of Armenians in the Ottoman Empire, 1915–16: Documents Presented to Viscount Grey of Fallondon, Secretary of State for Foreign Affairs*, Forgotten Books, 2017

Comment and notes on defeat of the French at Marash in 1920 can be found in Cabinet papers at the British National Archives in Kew, reference CAB 24/154. Other letters about the Armenians by Bryce include FO 800/105/102, FO 800/105/105. British investigations into Turkish massacres post-war are also detailed in FO 608/247/3 and references to the war crimes trials as well as massacres in Urfa in FO 608/78/4. Communication regarding the massacre at Marash in 1920 can be found in FO 608/275/11.

SECONDARY LITERATURE

The American Committee for Relief in the Near East, The American Committee for Relief in the Near East its history, its work and the need for support as outlined by President Wilson and others, Self-published pamphlet, 1918

Akcam, Taner, *A Shameful Act: The Armenian Genocide and the Question of Turkish Responsibility*, Henry Holt and Company, 2006

Balakian, Peter, *The Burning Tigris, The Armenian Genocide and America's Response*, HarperCollins, 2003

Bloxham, Donald, *The Great Game of Genocide: Imperialism, Nationalism, and the Destruction of the Ottoman Armenians*, Oxford University Press, 2005

Brown, Carl, L., *International Politics and the Middle East: Old Rules, Dangerous Game*, Princeton University Press, 1984

Bournoutian, George A., *A Concise History of the Armenian People*, Mazda publishers, 2002

Chatty, Dawn, *Displacement and Dispossession in the Modern Middle East*, Cambridge University Press, 2010

Cheterian, Vicken, *Open Wounds: Armenians, Turks, and a century of Genocide*, C. Hurst & Co., 2015

Vahakn Dadrian's excellent research into the Armenian Genocide trials which began in 1919, provides a detailed look at the evidence presented, the judicial process and how it was reported. The reaction to the trials within Turkey itself and particularly in the Constantinople press was not uniformly critical. Early on, there was widespread support for the idea of holding the CUP leadership to account for Turkey's post-war predicament, although not necessarily for the treatment of the Armenians. This book is simply too short to permit an in-depth and nuanced analysis of the machinations of the Turkish politics that led to the rise of Ataturk and the creation of modern Turkey and therefore I have had to content myself with a simple narration of the facts of history and how they related the Armenian question. The trials unravelled because of several factors, but primarily it was because the assertion of the British Foreign Secretary, Lord Curzon, that Turkey was "a culprit awaiting sentence" was rejected outright by the Turkish population. Having been promised victory over their enemies at the outbreak of the war by the CUP leaders, post-war they were disinclined to accept the de facto position of losers:

Dadrian Vahakn N. & Akçam, Taner, *Judgment at Istanbul: The Armenian Genocide Trials*, Berghahn Books, 2011

Dadrian, Vahakn N., *The Armenian Genocide: Review of its Historical, Political and Legal Aspects*, University of St. Thomas Journal of Law and Public Policy Volume 5 Issue 1, Fall 2010

Demirdjian, Alexis, *The Armenian Genocide Legacy*, Palgrave Macmillan, 2016

Durie, Mark, *The Third Choice, Islam, Dhimmitude and Freedom*, Deror Books, 2010

Emon, Anver, M., *Religious Pluralism and Islamic Law, Dhimmis and Others in the Empire of Law*, Oxford Islamic Legal Studies, Oxford University Press, 2014

Fierro, Maribel & Tolan, John, *The legal status of Dimmi-s in the Islamic West (Second/eighth-Ninth/Fifteenth Centuries)*, Brepols Publishers, 2013

Ataturk's initial attitude toward the Armenians appears at first to be somewhat sympathetic. Early on, he came out in support of the war crimes trials of the CUP leaders, even referring to the massacres as "criminal acts". However, the later actions of the government he led suggest that his statement of support were little more than criticism of the former administration. Under Ataturk, the Turkish government not only swiftly abolished the war crimes trials, but the following year decreed that the property of all Armenians who had fled the country would be confiscated by the state if not claimed within three months:

Hanioglu, M., Sukru, *Ataturk, An intellectual Biography*, Princeton University Press, 2011

Hovannisian, Richard G. & Payaslian, Simon, *Armenian Cilicia*, Mazda Publishers, 2008

Hovannisian, Richard G, *Remembrance and Denial, The Case of the Armenian Genocide*, Wayne State University Press, 1999

Jongerden, Joost & Verheij, Jelle, *Social Relations in Ottoman Diyarbekir, 1870-1915*, Brill, 2012

Guclu, Yucel, *Historical Archives and the Historians'Commission to Investigate the Armenian Events of 1915*, University Press of America, 2015

Grigor Suny, Ronald, Müge Göçek, Fatma & Naimark Norman M., *A Question of Genocide: Armenians and Turks at the End of the Ottoman Empire*, Oxford University Press, USA, 2011

Heller, Kevin & Simpson, Gerry, *The Hidden Histories of War Crimes Trials*, Oxford University Press, 2014

Stefan Ihrig's first work on Ataturk briefly considers the influence on the Turkish nationalism and the Armenian genocide on the Holocaust. For an in-depth study see:

Ihrig, Stefan, *Ataturk in the Nazi Imagination*, Harvard University Press, 2014

_____, *Justifying Genocide: Germany and the Armenians from Bismarck to Hitler*, Harvard University Press, 2016

For an extremely detailed overview of the Genocide, which examines each of the different *vilayets* and the deportations and massacres of Armenians in each, see Raymond Kevorkian's 1,000-page analysis:

Kevorkian, Raymond, *The Armenian Genocide, A Complete History*, I. B.Tauris, 2011

Kieser, H. L., *From 'Patriotism' to Mass Murder: Dr. Mehmed Reşid (1873–1919)*, University of Zurich, Zurich Open Repository & Archive, 2011

Kinross, Patrick Baron Balfour, *The Ottoman Centuries, The Rise and Fall of the Turkish Empire*, Morrow, 1977

There are many books about the Armenian people, but few written as hauntingly as Philip Marsden's part history, part travel memoir, *The Crossing Place*:

Marsden, Philip, *The Crossing Place: A Journey Among the Armenians*, William Collins, 2015

Mayersen, Deborah, *On the Path to Genocide, Armenia and Rwanda Re-examined*, Berghahan Books, 2014

Marriot, Sir John A., *The Eastern Question: An Historical Study in European Diplomacy*, Clarendon Press, 1940

Doctor Fred Shepard's wife, Alice, wrote an account of her and husband's experiences working as missionaries in Turkey. In it, she narrates Dr Shepard's work with the Armenians during the Genocide:

Riggs, Shepard, Alice, *Shepard of Aintab*, Interchurch Press, 1920

Stillman, Norman, A., (ed), *Encylcopedia of Jews in the Islamic World, Volume Two D-I*, Brill, 2010

Quataert, Donald & Inalcik, Halil, *An Economic and Social History of the Ottoman Empire, 1300–1914*, Cambridge University Press, 1994

Ungur, Ugor & Polatel, *Mehmet, Confiscation and Destruction: the Young Turk Seizure of Armenian Property*, Continuum Books, 2011

Wilmshurst, David, *The Martyred Church, A History of the Church of the East*, East & East Publishing Ltd, 2011

Winter, Jay, *America and the Armenian Genocide of 1915*, Cambridge University Press, 2003

Ye'or, Bat, *Islam and Dhimmitude: Where Civilisations Collide*, Associated University Press, 2002

_____, *The Decline of Eastern Christianity Under Islam: From Jihad to Dhimmitude*, Associated University Press, 1996

THE ASSYRIAN AND PONTIC GENOCIDES

Hofmann, Bjornlund & Meichanetsidis, Vasileios, *The Genocide of the Ottoman Greeks: Studies on the State-sponsored Campaign of Extermination of the Christians of Asia Minor (1912–1922) and its Aftermath: History, Law, Memory*, Melissa International Ltd., 2011

Joseph, John, *The Nestorians and their Muslim Neighbours: A Study of Western Influence on Their relations*, Princeton University Press, 1961

Papoutsy, Christos, *Ships of Mercy: The True Story of the Rescue of the Greeks, Smyrna, September 1922*, Peter E. Randell Publisher LLC, 2008

The best single resource on the Assyrian Genocide is Joseph Yacoub's account, which includes excellent references to useful primary sources. It was published in English in 2016:

Yacoub Joseph, *Year of the Sword, The Assyrian Christian Genocide, A History*, C. Hurst & Co (Publishers) Ltd., 2016

Picture Credits

Henry Morgenthau portrait; Library of Congress, Prints & Photographs Division, photograph by Harris & Ewing, [LC-USZ62-93469]

U.S. Embassy in Constantinople; Library of Congress, Prints & Photographs Division, [LC-DIG-ggbain-21098]

Galata Bridge; Library of Congress, Prints & Photographs Division, [LC-USZ62-137703]

Mehmed Talaat; Library of Congress, Prints & Photographs Division, [LC-DIG-ggbain-31323]

Widowed Armenian woman; Library of Congress, Prints & Photographs Division, [LC-DIG-ggbain-27081]

Refugees at Aintab; Library of Congress, Prints & Photographs Division, [LC-DIG-ggbain-27084]

Dolmabahçe Palace; Library of Congress, Prints & Photographs Division, [LC-DIG-ggbain-18565]

Ismail Enver; Library of Congress, Prints & Photographs Division, [LC-USZ62-77293]

Jesse B. Jackson; Library of Congress, Prints & Photographs Division, photograph by Harris & Ewing, [LC-DIG-hec-18934]

Armenian orphans boarding ship; Library of Congress, Prints & Photographs Division, [LC-USZ62-93055]

Armenian woman and child; Library of Congress, Prints & Photographs Division, [LC-USZ62-48100]

1917 appeal poster; Library of Congress, Prints & Photographs Division, WWI Posters, [LC-DIG-ppmsca-50553]

Morgenthau and Dodge; Library of Congress, Prints & Photographs Division, [LC-DIG-ggbain-21106]

Forty slaughtered Armenians; Library of Congress, Prints & Photographs Division, [LC-DIG-ds-01042]

British troops marching by Nusretiye Mosque in the Tophane district of Istanbul; Library of Congress, Prints & Photograph Division, [LC-USZ62-139313]

German workers building stations at Aleppo for the Baghdad Railway: Library of Congress, Prints & Photograph Division, [LC-DIG-matpc-04669]

Photograph obtained by the American Red Cross, Library of Congress, Prints & Photograph Division, [LC-DIG-ds-01042]

Armenian orphans begging in Russia. *Library of Congress, Prints & Photographs Division, American National Red Cross Collection,* [LC-DIG-anrc-05468]

Armenian street children, mid-1920s. *Fridtjof Nansen/ National Library of Norway*

Armenian village women from Hawadorig, pre-1917, in deepest winter; Starving Armenian children. *Bodil Biørn/ National Archives of Norway*

Armenians defending Van; Armenians marched to prison; Baron von Wangenheim; Those who fell by the wayside; Bones of those massacred near Erzerum; SS George Washington; Turkish soldiers in Constantinople at the declaration; Kurdish cavalry; Erzerum blanketed with snow; Armenian orphanage in Aleppo, 1920; Armenian resistance at Urfa; A caravan of 5,000 Greek Orthodox refugees; Mustafa Kenal Ataturk; Sohhomon Tehlirian; Armenian Genocide memorial church in Der-el-Zor; Armenian women, as depicted in the late 19th century; Armenian women in Borjomi, Georgia, 1912; Armenian women fedayi (militia), 1918; Deportations of Armenians. The man in the foreground is a gendarme; Turkish troops and a military band on a parade ground; Skulls of Armenians massacred at Urfa, surrounded by Armenian dignitaries and women from the women's shelter in Urfa's Monastery of St Sarkis, June 1919; Armenian refugees rescued by a French cruiser, 1915; Armenian refugees receiving food relief from the American Committee for Relief in the Near East, 1916; Armenian refugee children in Gyumri, Armenia, circa 1919; An Armenian woman in traditional dress, poses on a hillside in Artvin, c. 1910; Armenian women from Gandzak (Azerbaijan), pre-1917; Turkish troops in action at the battle of Qatia, Sinai, where they defeated the British in 1915; Military supplies piled up at Anzac Cove, Gallipoli, May 1915; V Beach at Helles, Gallipoli; The Young Turks enter Constantinople, 1909; After the comprehensive defeat by the Russians at Sarikamish, desperate Turkish stragglers make for Erzerum, October 1914; Armenians with spinning wheels and cotton, Erivan, c. 1915; Armenian refugee children paddling in the sea near Marathon, Greece, c. 1915; Armenian refugees in Marsovan, Turkey, near the Black Sea; Armenian orphans at a Near East Relief facility in Syria; A Near East Relief camp in the Turkish countryside, December 1919; Armenian children in Baghdad, 1918; An Armenian and Syrian Relief Campaign fundraising poster; The text on the left-hand-side reads: "Taken: 3/8/1919: ARMENIAN REFUGEES WHO ARRIVED IN UNITED STATES. Armenian refugees who were among the most prosperous families of Harpoot and who fled Turkey to escape the atrocities of Turks. The party which arrived at San Francisco, is led by Sooren Darkaspirin, a nineteen year old lad, [the] only [one] of [the] party who speaks the English language, is second from the right."; An Armenian and Syrian Relief Campaign fundraising poster; Four Armenian women photographed at a rescue home in the early 1920s, having just escaped slavery. Their relief is palpable; Lady Anne Azgapetian, wife of General Azgapetian, of Armenia, with her daughter Araxia, at the convention of the National Woman's Party in Washington DC, February 1921. *Wikimedia Commons*

Index

David Charlwood obtained a First Class Honours degree in history from Royal Holloway, University of London, and has worked as a writer and international journalist since 2012. His research into the early twentieth-century Middle East has been published in the *British Journal of Middle Eastern Studies*. David writes for the Pen & Sword series 'History of Terror' and 'Cold War 1945–1991'.

Coming soon from David Charlwood

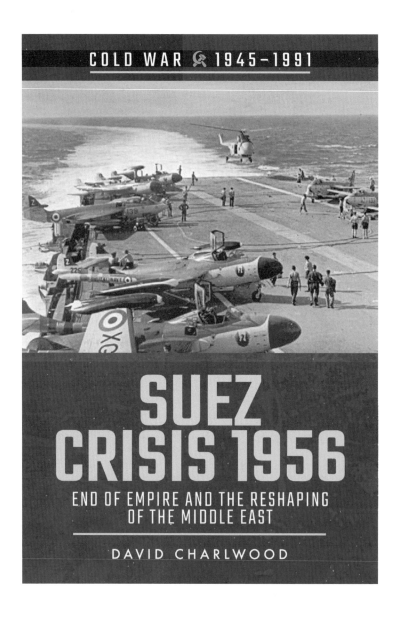

COLD WAR ☭ 1945–1991

SUEZ CRISIS 1956

END OF EMPIRE AND THE RESHAPING OF THE MIDDLE EAST

DAVID CHARLWOOD